The California Gold Rush

written by
Joe Dunn
illustrated by
Ben Dunn

magic
wagon

visit us at
www.abdopublishing.com

Published by Magic Wagon, a division of the ABDO Publishing Group, 8000 West 78th Street, Edina, Minnesota 55439. Copyright © 2008 by Abdo Consulting Group, Inc. International copyrights reserved in all countries. All rights reserved. No part of this book may be reproduced in any form without written permission from the publisher. Graphic Planet™ is a trademark and logo of Magic Wagon.

Printed in the United States of America, North Mankato, Minnesota.

Written by Joe Dunn
Illustrated by Ben Dunn
Colored by Robby Bevard
Lettered by Joe Dunn
Edited by Stephanie Hedlund
Interior layout and design by Antarctic Press
Cover art by Ben Dunn and GURU-eFX
Cover design by Neil Klinepier

Library of Congress Cataloging-in-Publication Data

Dunn, Joeming W.
    The California Gold Rush / Joe Dunn; illustrated by Ben Dunn.
    p. cm. -- (Graphic history)
    Includes index.
    ISBN 978-1-60270-076-5
    1. California--Gold discoveries--Juvenile literature. 2. Frontier and pioneer life--California--Juvenile literature. 3. Sutter, John Augustus, 1803-1880--Juvenile literature. 4. Pioneers--California--Biography--Juvenile literature. 5. California--History--1846-1850--Juvenile literature. 6. Graphic novels. I. Dunn, Ben. II. Title.

F865.D92 2008
979.4'04--dc22

012008
042010

2007006438

TABLE of CONTENTS

Timeline

1804 - President Thomas Jefferson chartered the Lewis and Clark Expedition, which opened the gateway to the West.

1846 - The city of Yerba Buena was established. It would later become San Francisco.

January 24, 1848 - During construction of a sawmill for John Sutter, gold was discovered by James Marshall.

February 2, 1848 - Mexico gave control of California to the United States as part of the treaty of Guadalupe Hidalgo.

March 15, 1848 - The first newspaper article reported the gold discovery.

May 12, 1848 - Samuel Brannan started the gold rush by shouting "Gold! Gold!" in the streets of San Francisco.

December 5, 1848 - President Polk confirmed gold findings during an address to Congress.

1849 - Several large steamships and wagon trains arrived bringing miners.

1850 - People started leaving due to a shortage of gold and an overabundance of miners.

September 9, 1850 - California was admitted to the United States as the 31st state.

1852 - Hydraulic mining began, with underground mining following soon after.

December 1854 - The gold rush ended.

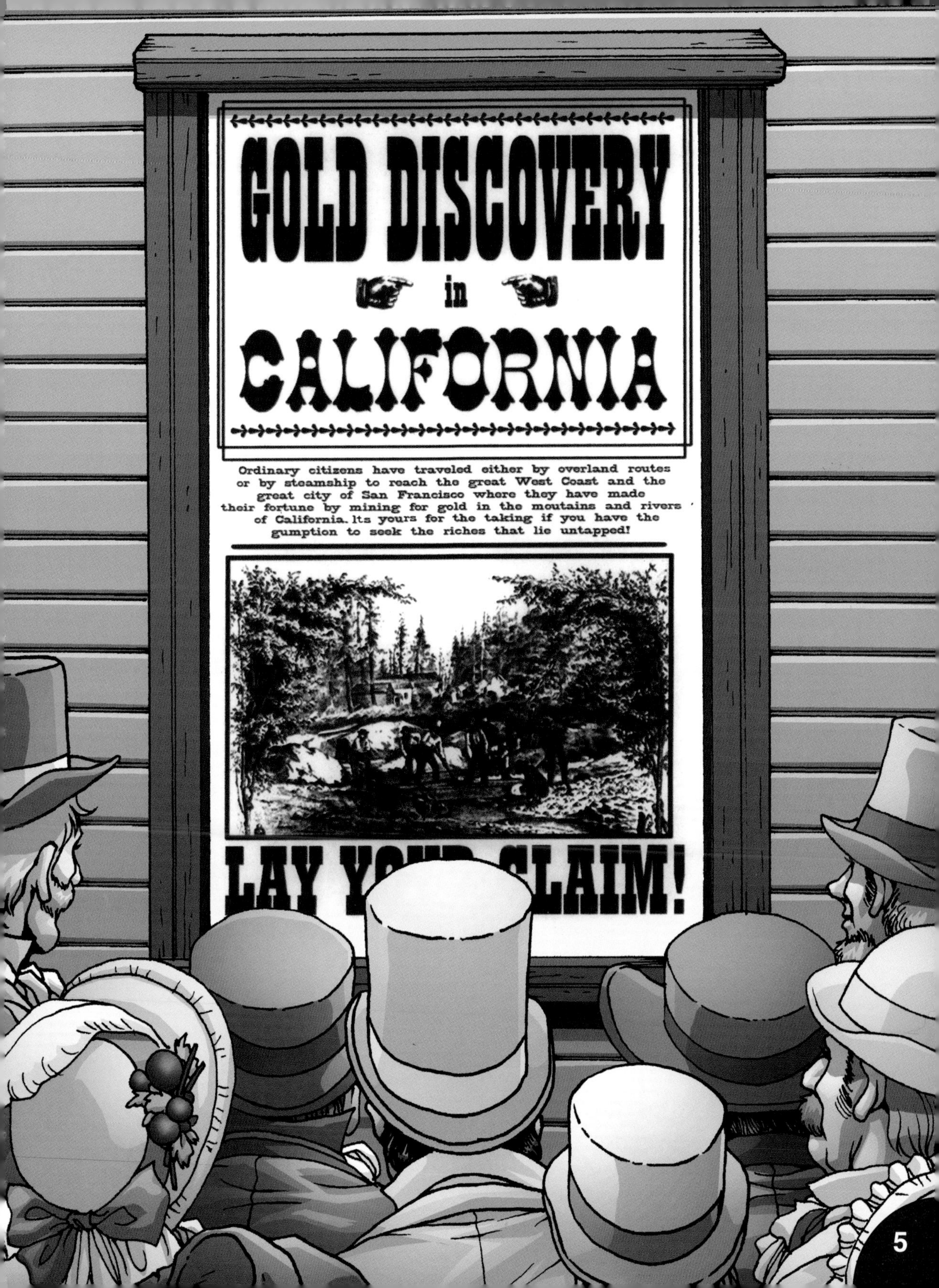
GOLD DISCOVERY
in
CALIFORNIA
Ordinary citizens have traveled either by overland routes or by steamship to reach the great West Coast and the great city of San Francisco where they have made their fortune by mining for gold in the moutains and rivers of California. Its yours for the taking if you have the gumption to seek the riches that lie untapped!
LAY
CLAIM!

Chapter 1 Heading West

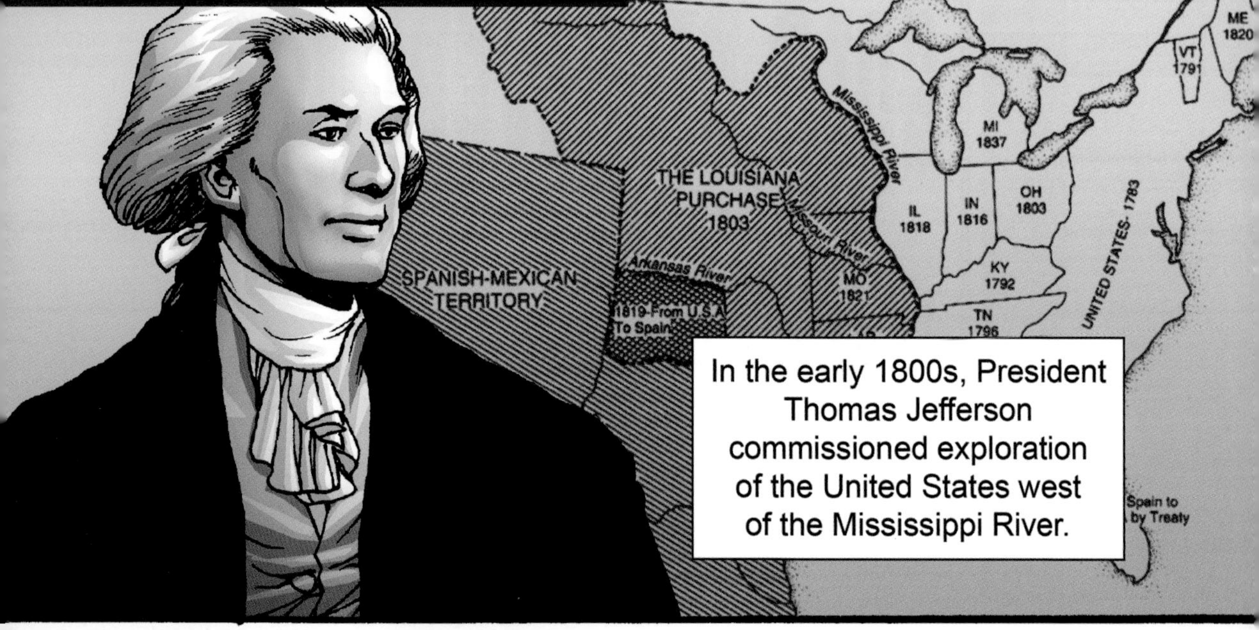

THE LOUISIANA PURCHASE 1803
SPANISH-MEXICAN TERRITORY
Arkansas River
1819-From U.S.A To Spain
Mississippi River
Missouri River
MO 1821
IL 1818
IN 1816
OH 1803
KY 1792
TN 1796
MI 1837
VT 1791
ME 1820
UNITED STATES- 1783
In the early 1800s, President Thomas Jefferson commissioned exploration of the United States west of the Mississippi River.

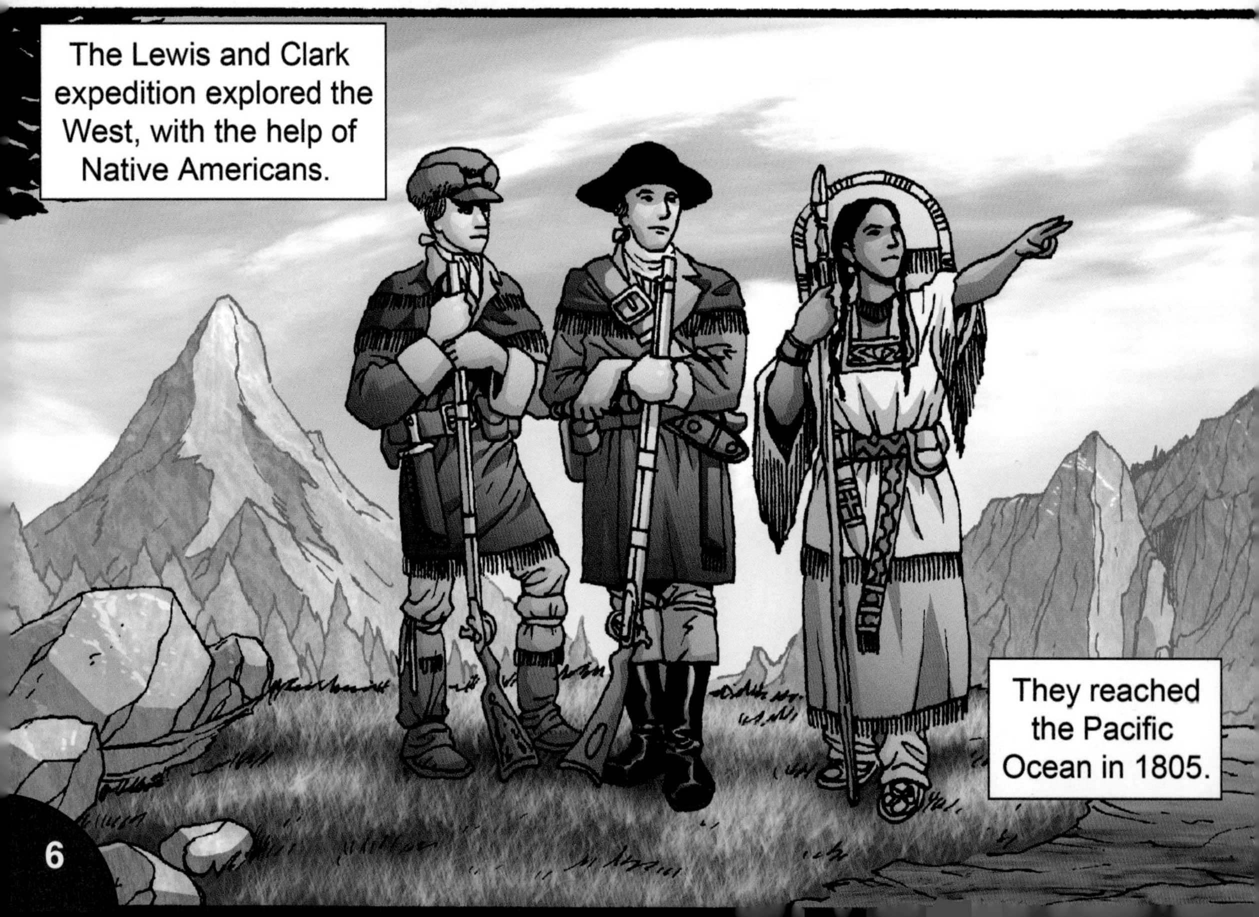

The Lewis and Clark expedition explored the West, with the help of Native Americans.
They reached the Pacific Ocean in 1805.

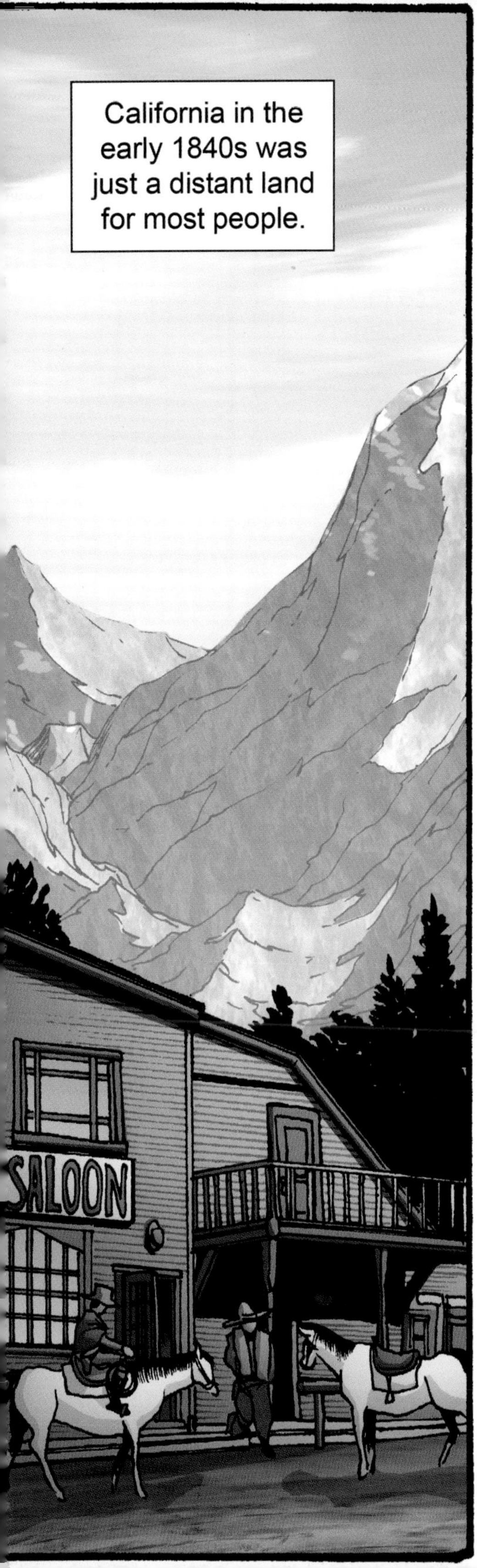
California in the early 1840s was just a distant land for most people.
SALOON

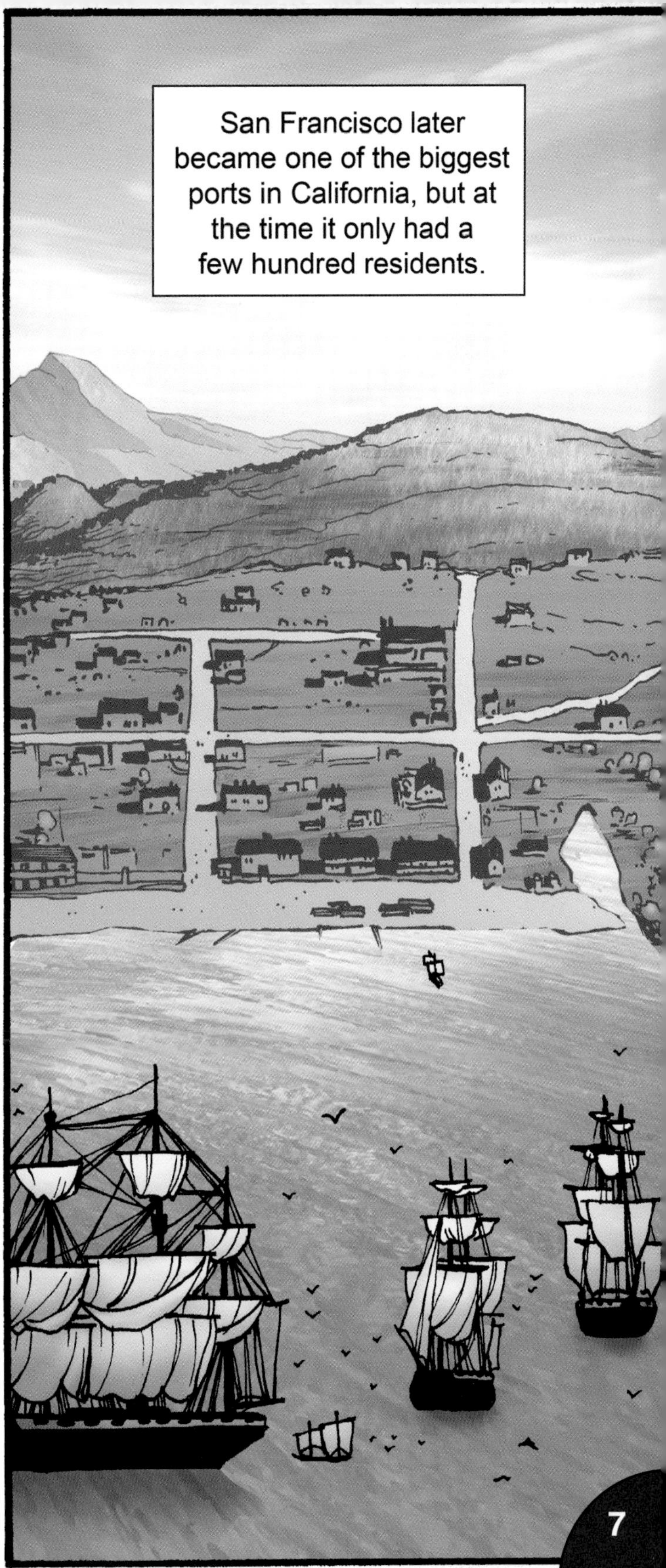
San Francisco later became one of the biggest ports in California, but at the time it only had a few hundred residents.

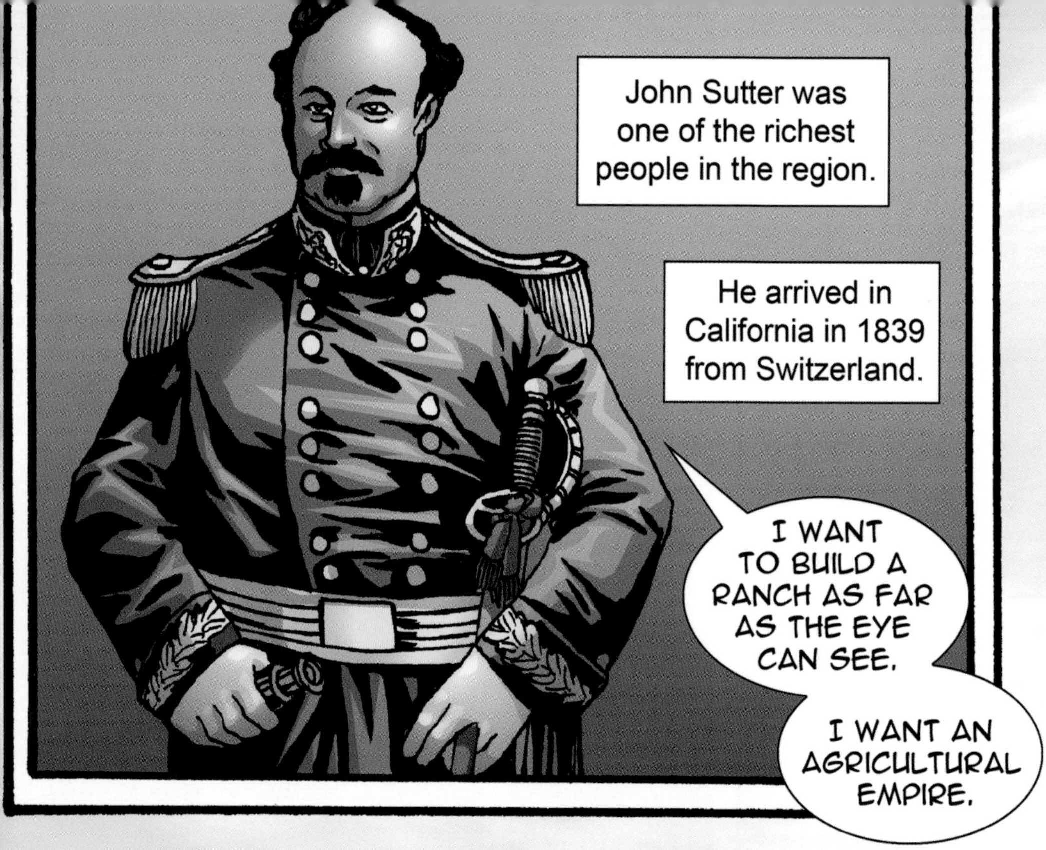
John Sutter was one of the richest people in the region.
He arrived in California in 1839 from Switzerland.
I WANT TO BUILD A RANCH AS FAR AS THE EYE CAN SEE.
I WANT AN AGRICULTURAL EMPIRE.

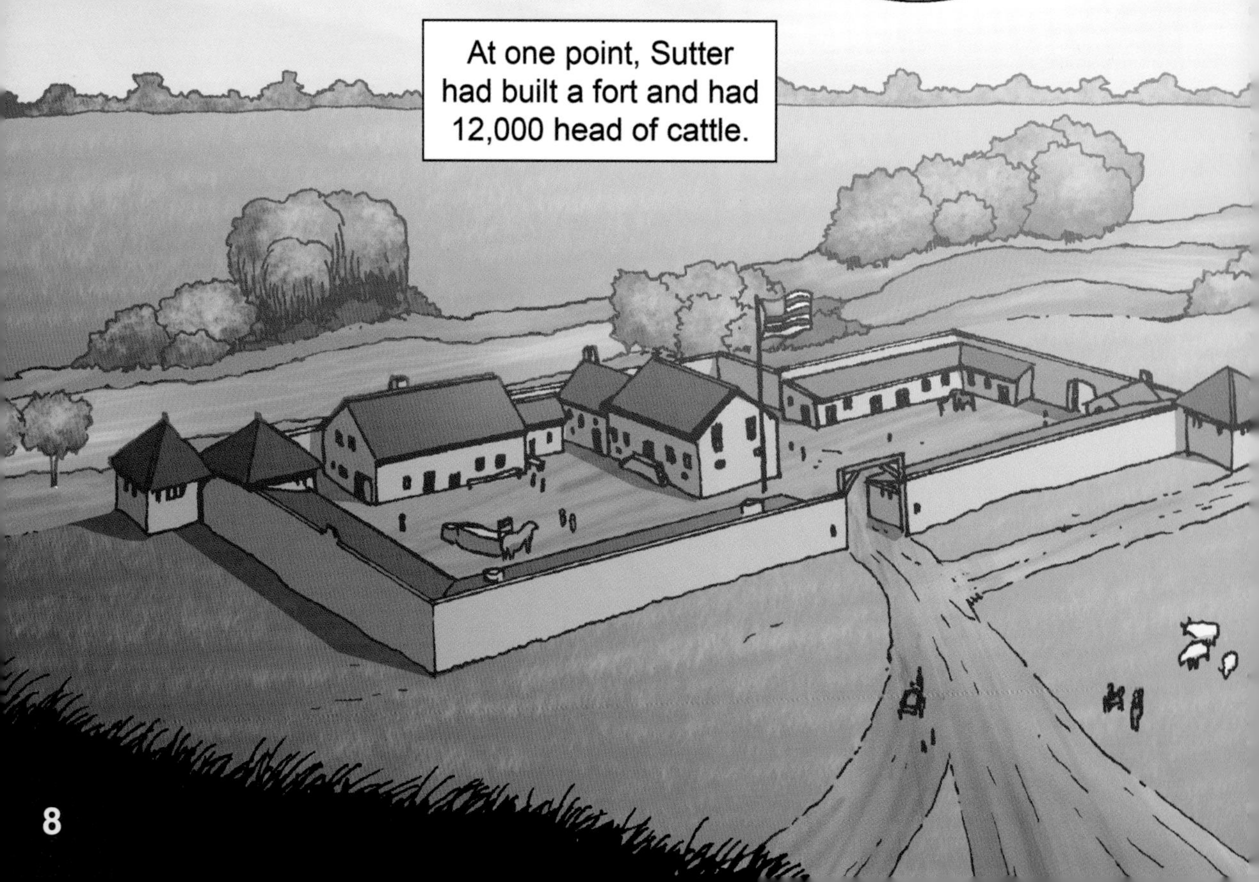
At one point, Sutter had built a fort and had 12,000 head of cattle.

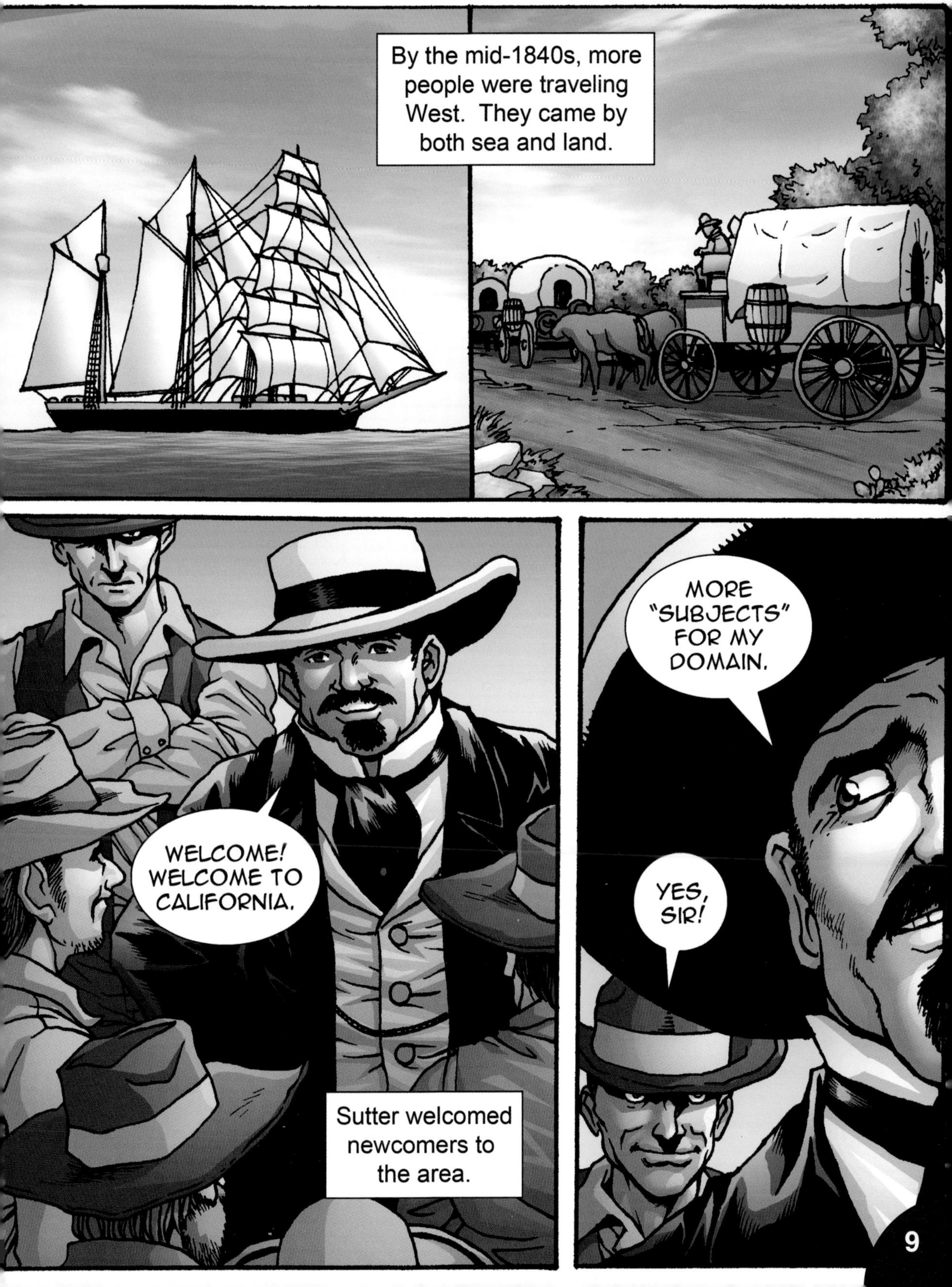
By the mid-1840s, more people were traveling West. They came by both sea and land.
WELCOME! WELCOME TO CALIFORNIA.
Sutter welcomed newcomers to the area.
MORE "SUBJECTS" FOR MY DOMAIN.
YES, SIR!

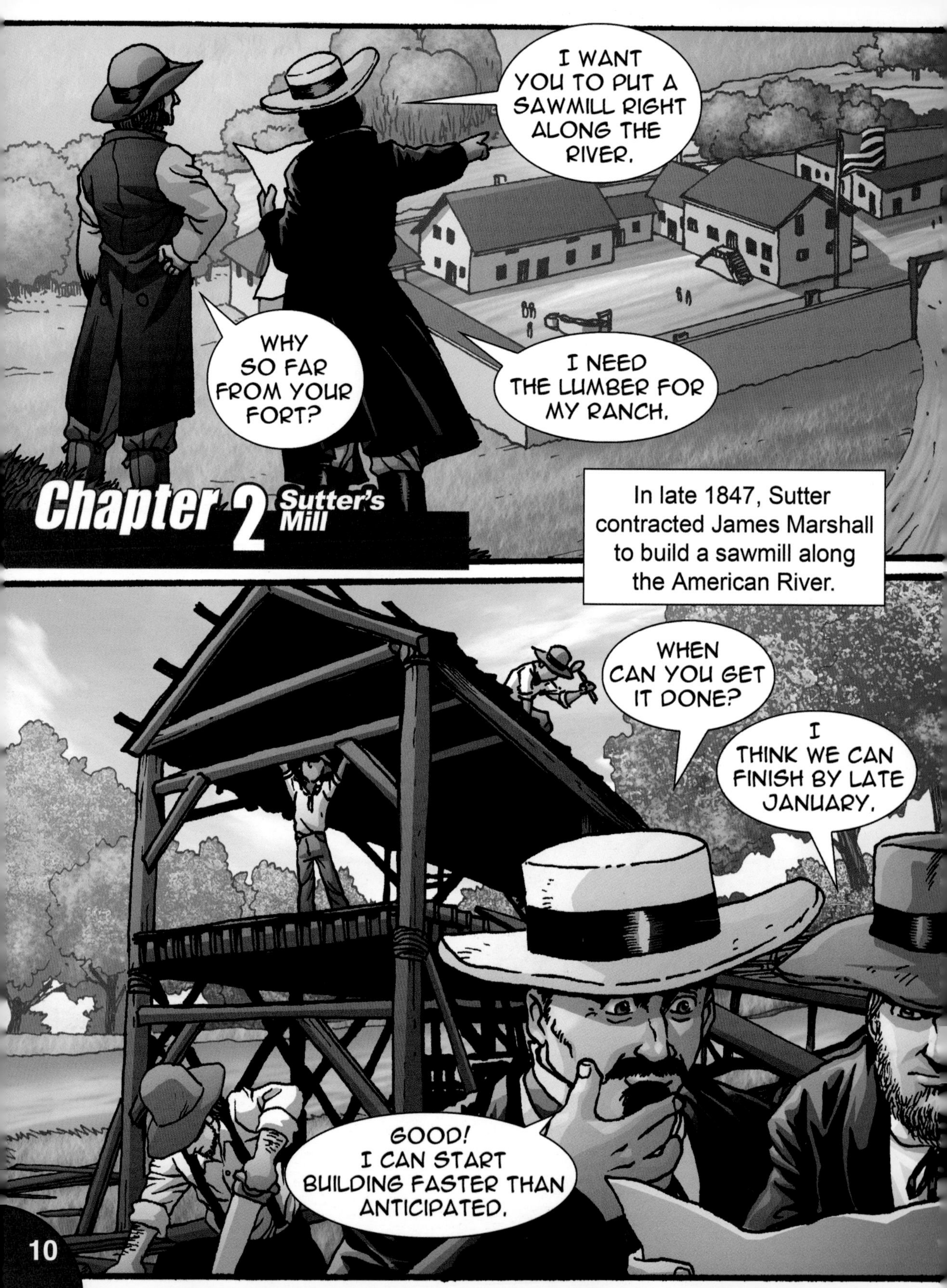
I WANT YOU TO PUT A SAWMILL RIGHT ALONG THE RIVER.
WHY SO FAR FROM YOUR FORT?
I NEED THE LUMBER FOR MY RANCH.
Chapter 2 Sutter's Mill
In late 1847, Sutter contracted James Marshall to build a sawmill along the American River.
WHEN CAN YOU GET IT DONE?
I THINK WE CAN FINISH BY LATE JANUARY.
GOOD! I CAN START BUILDING FASTER THAN ANTICIPATED.

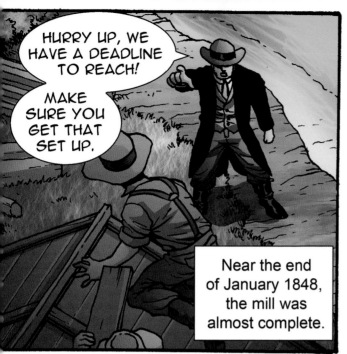

HURRY UP, WE HAVE A DEADLINE TO REACH!

MAKE SURE YOU GET THAT SET UP.

Near the end of January 1848, the mill was almost complete.

Then one day, something caught Marshall's eye.

WHAT IS THAT?

Marshall reached down and picked something up.

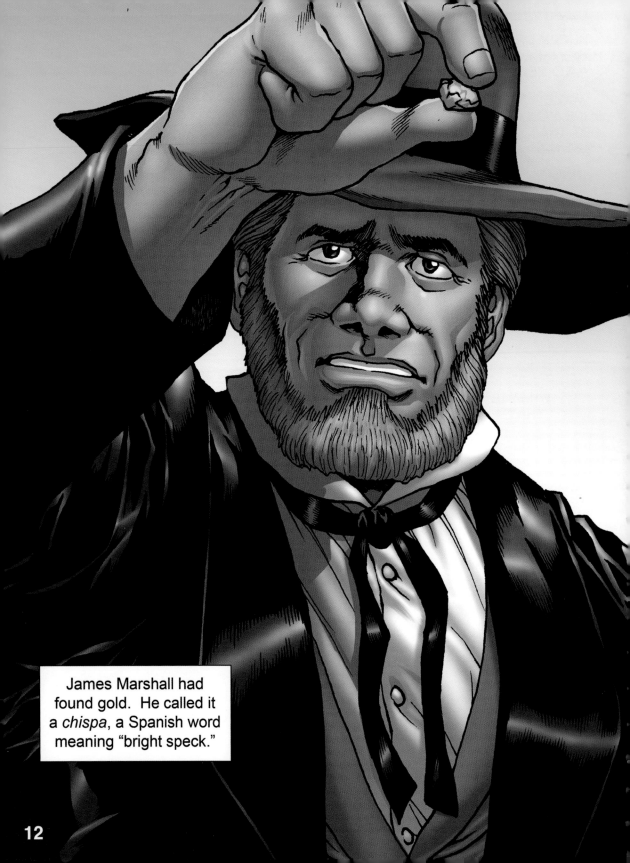

James Marshall had found gold. He called it a *chispa*, a Spanish word meaning "bright speck."

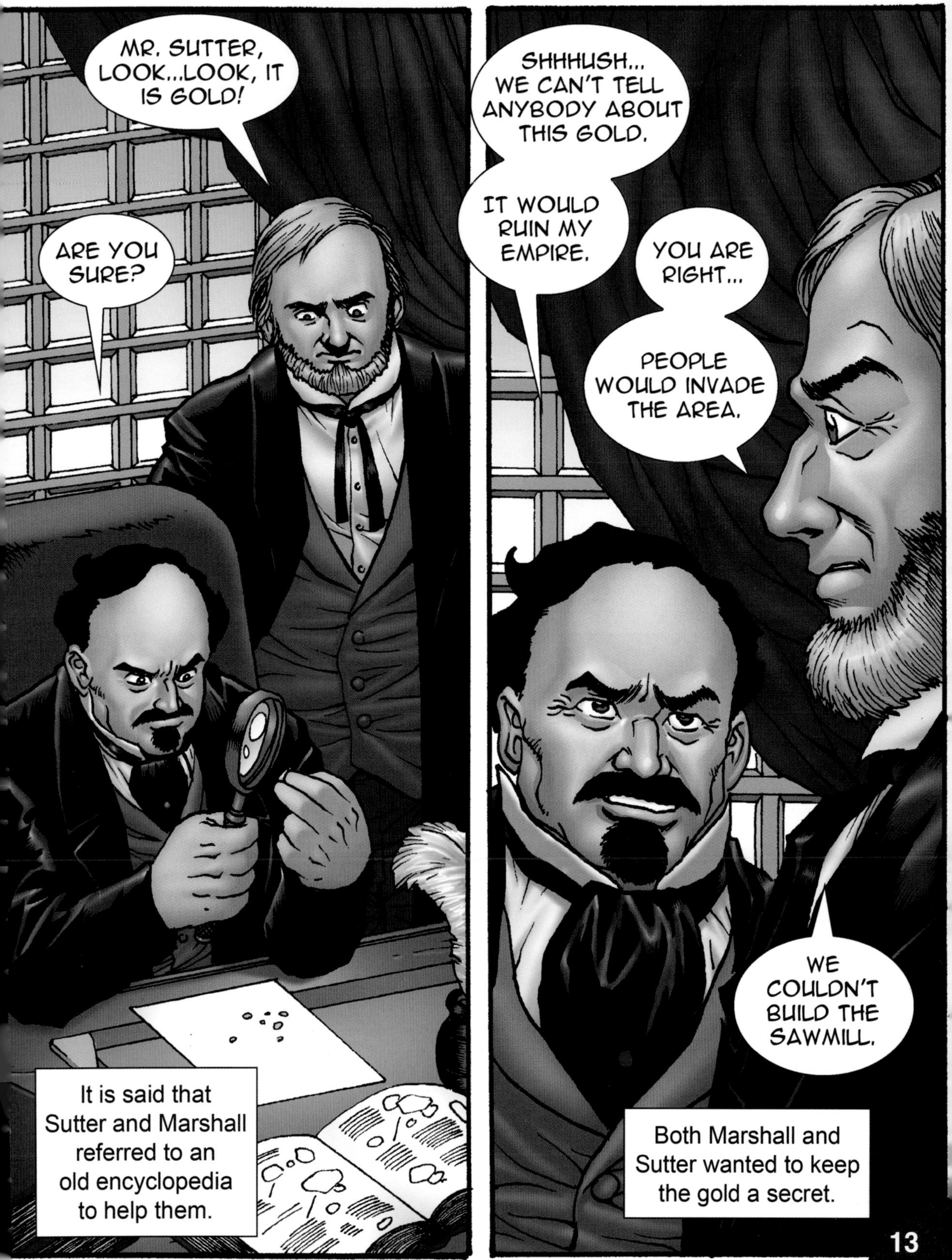
MR. SUTTER, LOOK...LOOK, IT IS GOLD!
ARE YOU SURE?
It is said that Sutter and Marshall referred to an old encyclopedia to help them.
SHHHUSH... WE CAN'T TELL ANYBODY ABOUT THIS GOLD.
IT WOULD RUIN MY EMPIRE.
YOU ARE RIGHT...
PEOPLE WOULD INVADE THE AREA.
WE COULDN'T BUILD THE SAWMILL.
Both Marshall and Sutter wanted to keep the gold a secret.

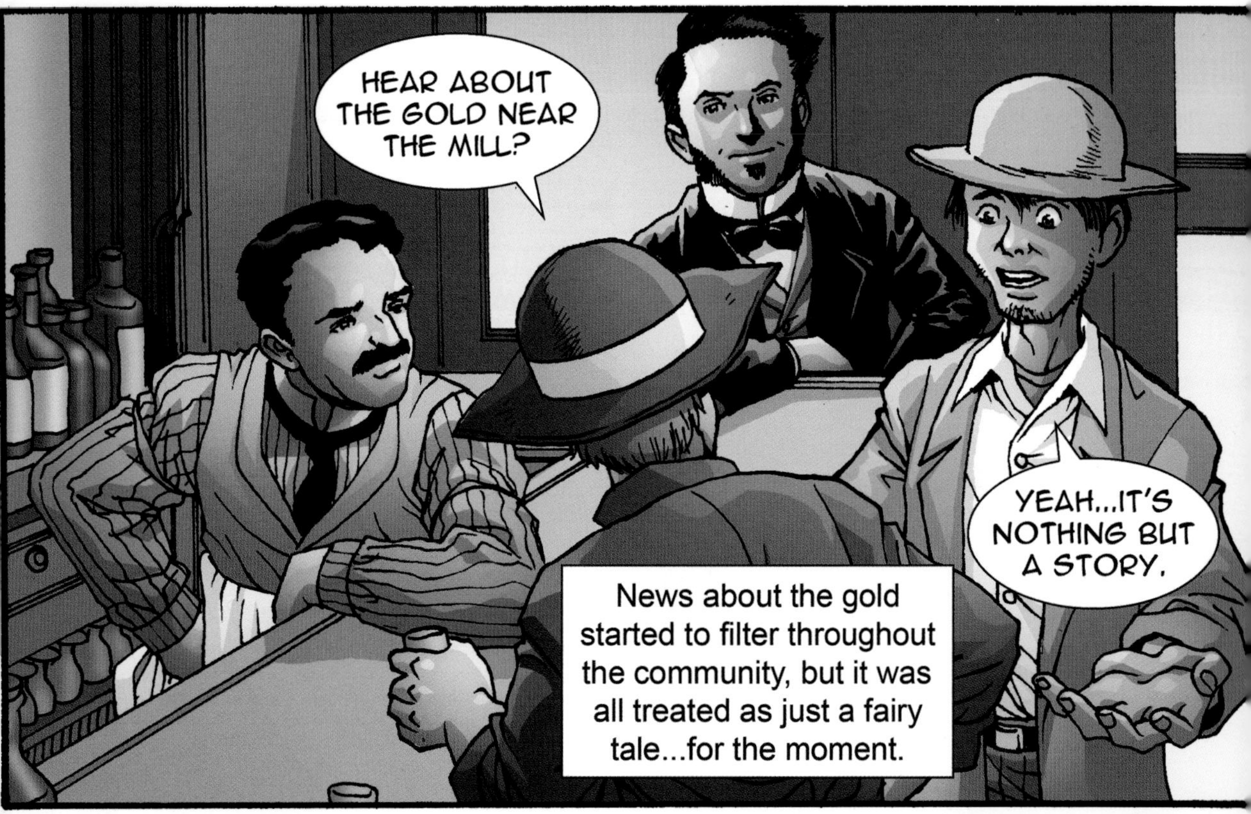
HEAR ABOUT THE GOLD NEAR THE MILL?
YEAH...IT'S NOTHING BUT A STORY.
News about the gold started to filter throughout the community, but it was all treated as just a fairy tale...for the moment.

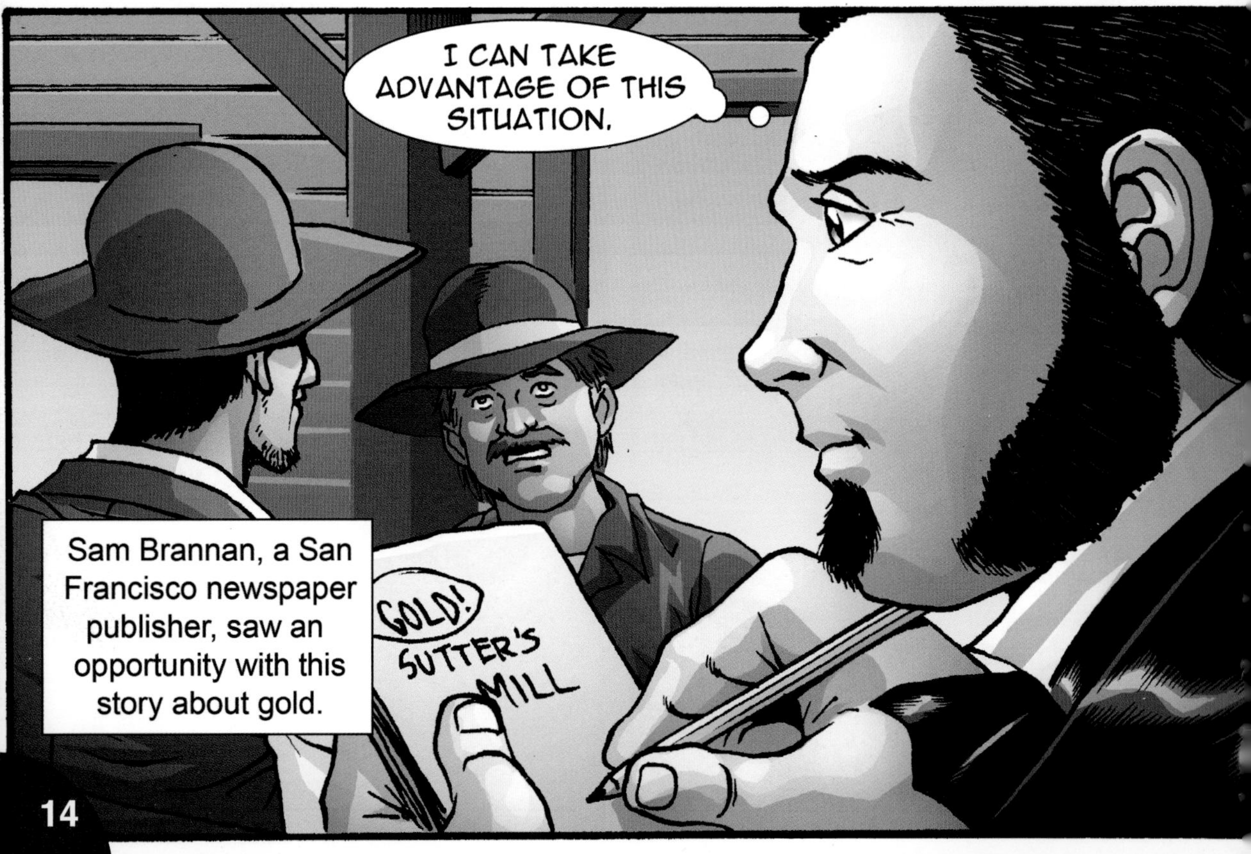
I CAN TAKE ADVANTAGE OF THIS SITUATION.
Sam Brannan, a San Francisco newspaper publisher, saw an opportunity with this story about gold.
GOLD!
SUTTER'S MILL

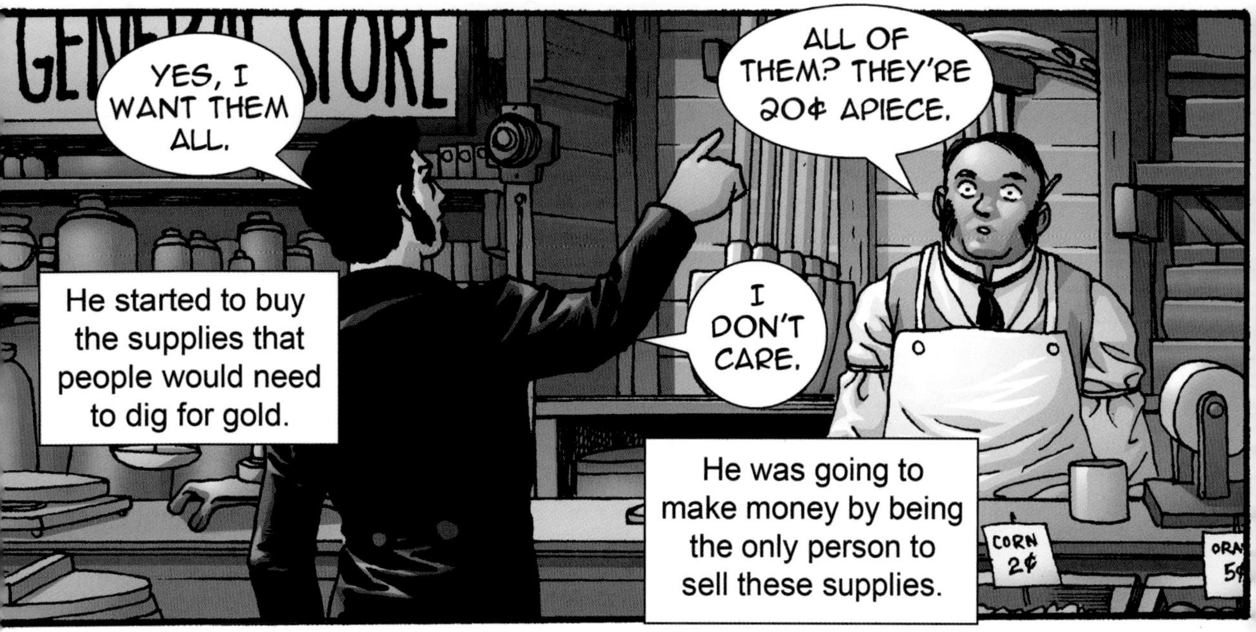
STORE
YES, I WANT THEM ALL.
ALL OF THEM? THEY'RE 20¢ APIECE.
I DON'T CARE.
He started to buy the supplies that people would need to dig for gold.
He was going to make money by being the only person to sell these supplies.
CORN 2¢

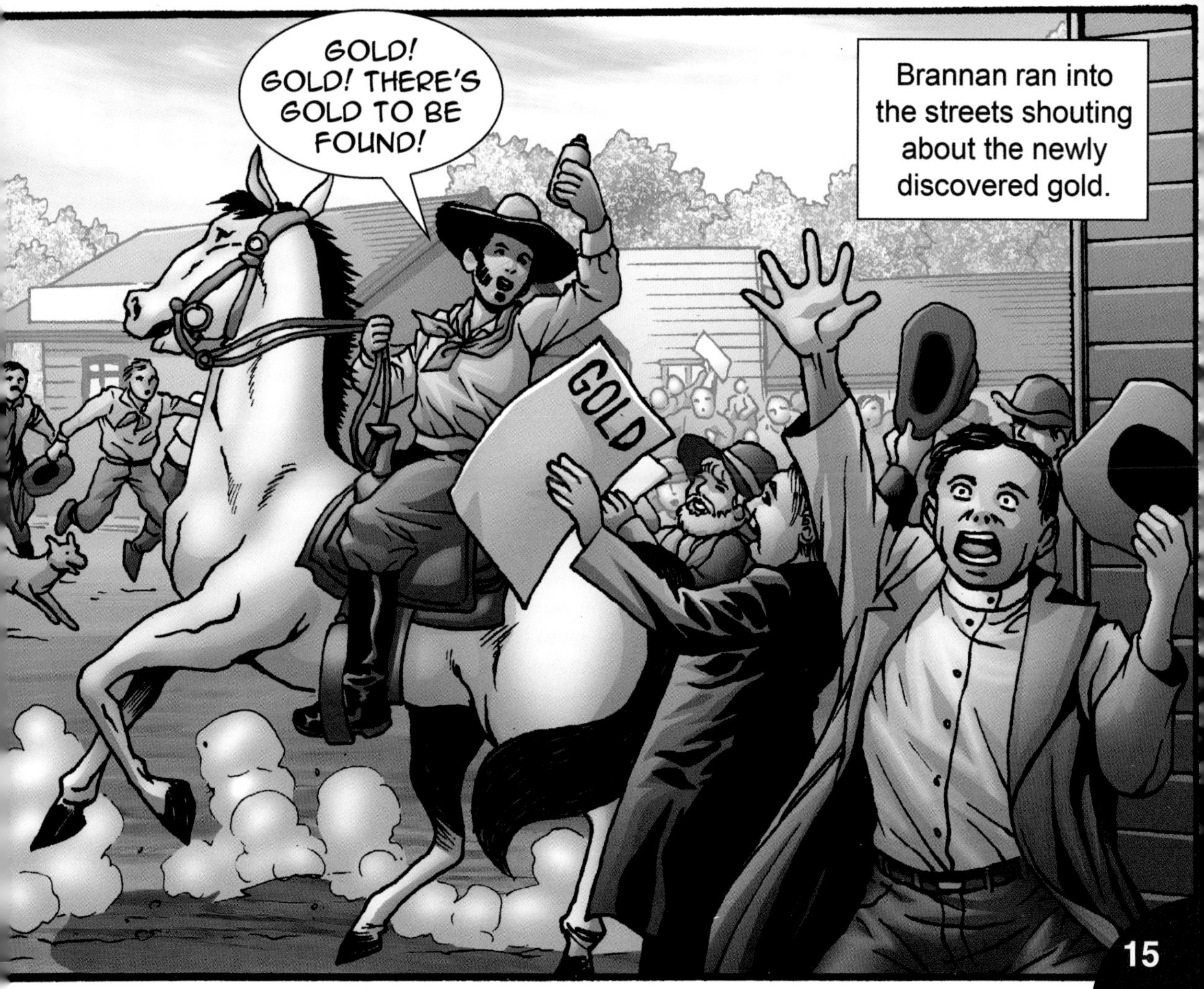
GOLD! GOLD! THERE'S GOLD TO BE FOUND!
Brannan ran into the streets shouting about the newly discovered gold.
GOLD

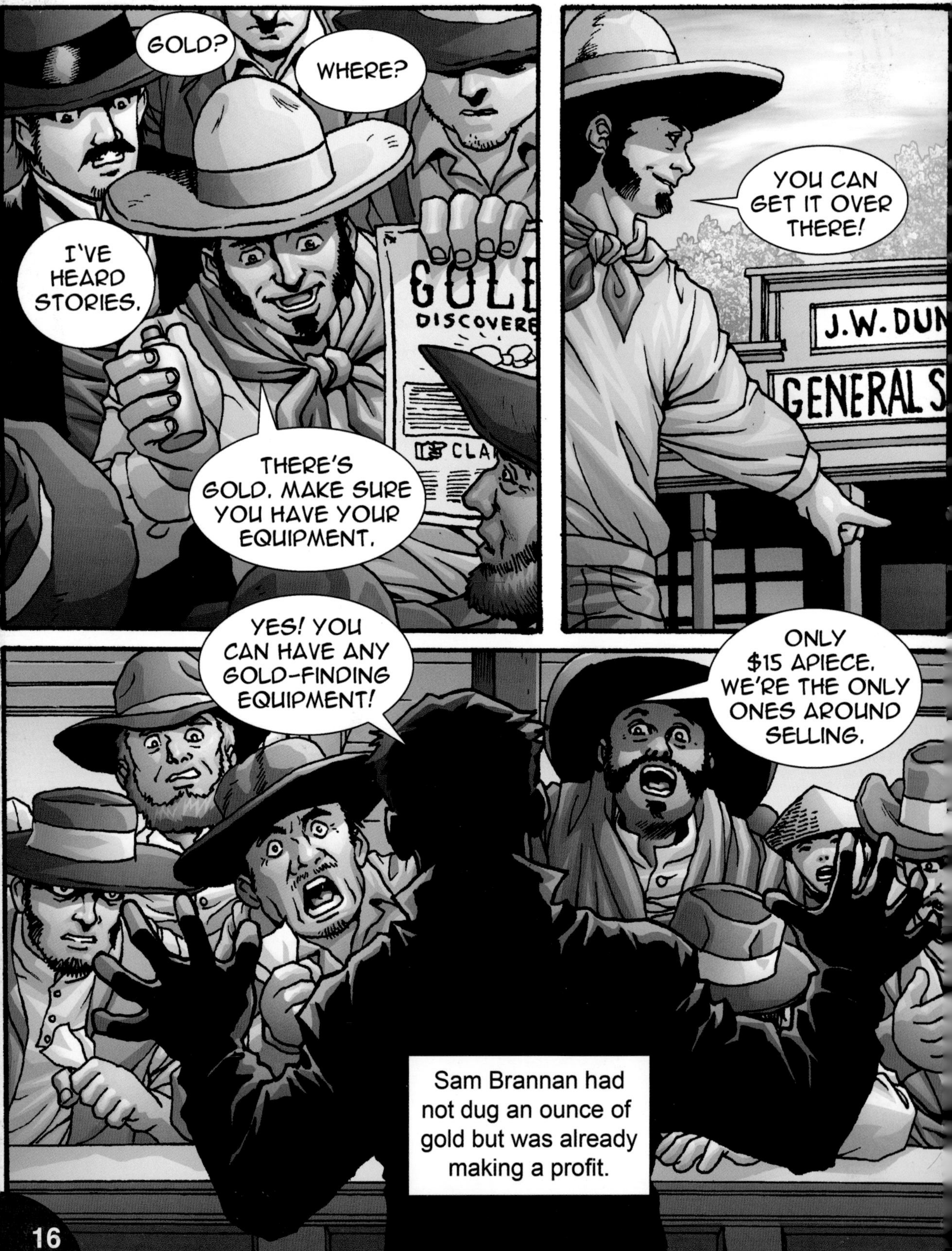
GOLD?
WHERE?
I'VE HEARD STORIES.
GOLD DISCOVERE
THERE'S GOLD. MAKE SURE YOU HAVE YOUR EQUIPMENT.
YOU CAN GET IT OVER THERE!
J.W. DUN
GENERAL S
YES! YOU CAN HAVE ANY GOLD-FINDING EQUIPMENT!
ONLY $15 APIECE. WE'RE THE ONLY ONES AROUND SELLING.
Sam Brannan had not dug an ounce of gold but was already making a profit.

Chapter 3 News Spreads

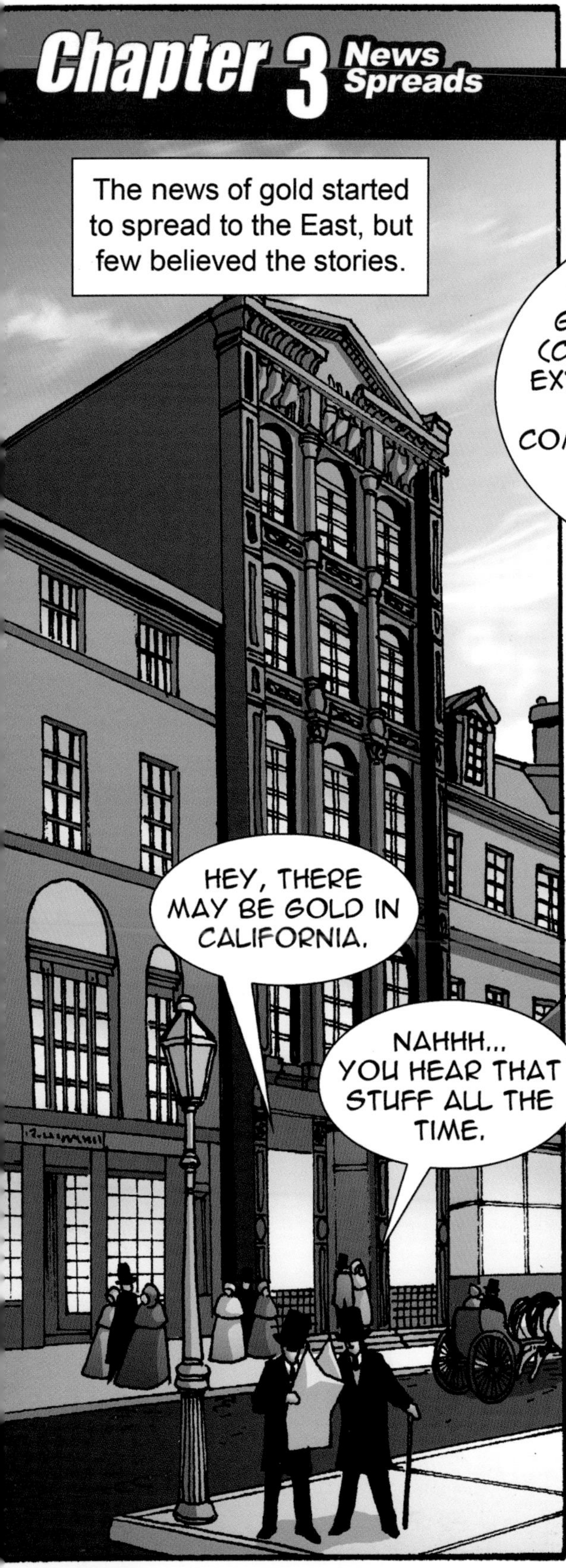

The news of gold started to spread to the East, but few believed the stories.
HEY, THERE MAY BE GOLD IN CALIFORNIA.
NAHHH... YOU HEAR THAT STUFF ALL THE TIME.

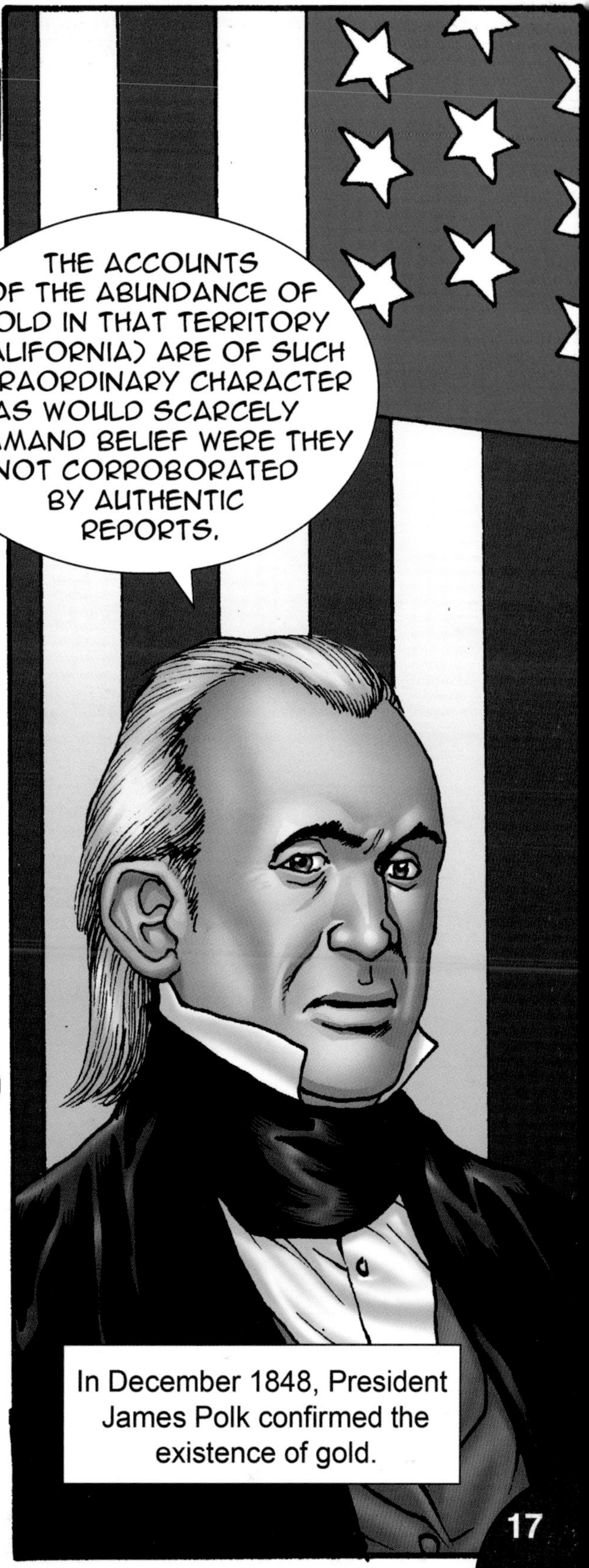

THE ACCOUNTS OF THE ABUNDANCE OF GOLD IN THAT TERRITORY (CALIFORNIA) ARE OF SUCH EXTRAORDINARY CHARACTER AS WOULD SCARCELY COMMAND BELIEF WERE THEY NOT CORROBORATED BY AUTHENTIC REPORTS.
In December 1848, President James Polk confirmed the existence of gold.

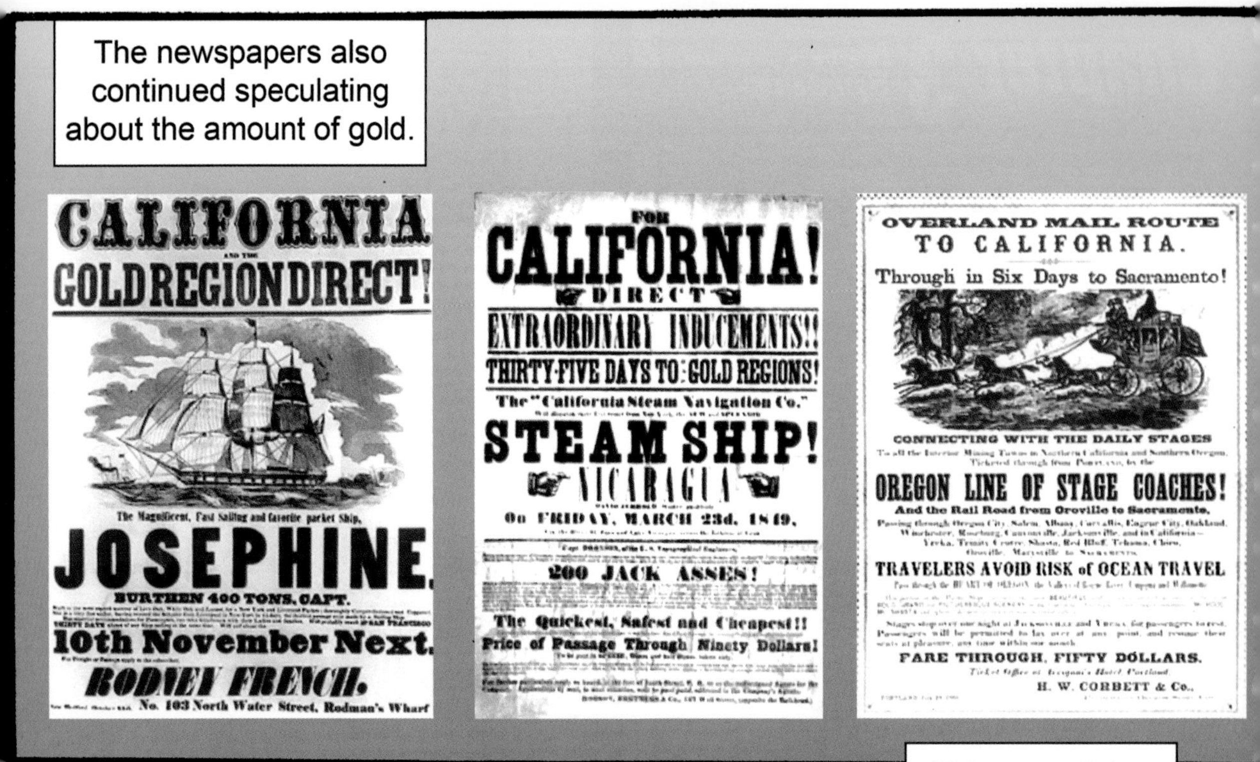

The newspapers also continued speculating about the amount of gold.
CALIFORNIA
GOLD REGION DIRECT!
The Magnificent, Fast Sailing and favorite packet Ship,
JOSEPHINE.
BURTHEN 400 TONS, CAPT.
10th November Next.
RODNEY FRENCH.
No. 103 North Water Street, Rodman's Wharf
FOR
CALIFORNIA!
DIRECT
EXTRAORDINARY INDUCEMENTS!!
THIRTY-FIVE DAYS TO GOLD REGIONS!
The "California Steam Navigation Co."
STEAM SHIP!
NICARAGUA
On FRIDAY, MARCH 23d, 1849,
200 JACK ASSES!
The Quickest, Safest and Cheapest!!
Price of Passage Through Ninety Dollars!
OVERLAND MAIL ROUTE
TO CALIFORNIA.
Through in Six Days to Sacramento!
CONNECTING WITH THE DAILY STAGES
OREGON LINE OF STAGE COACHES!
And the Rail Road from Oroville to Sacramento,
TRAVELERS AVOID RISK of OCEAN TRAVEL
FARE THROUGH, FIFTY DOLLARS.
H. W. CORBETT & Co.

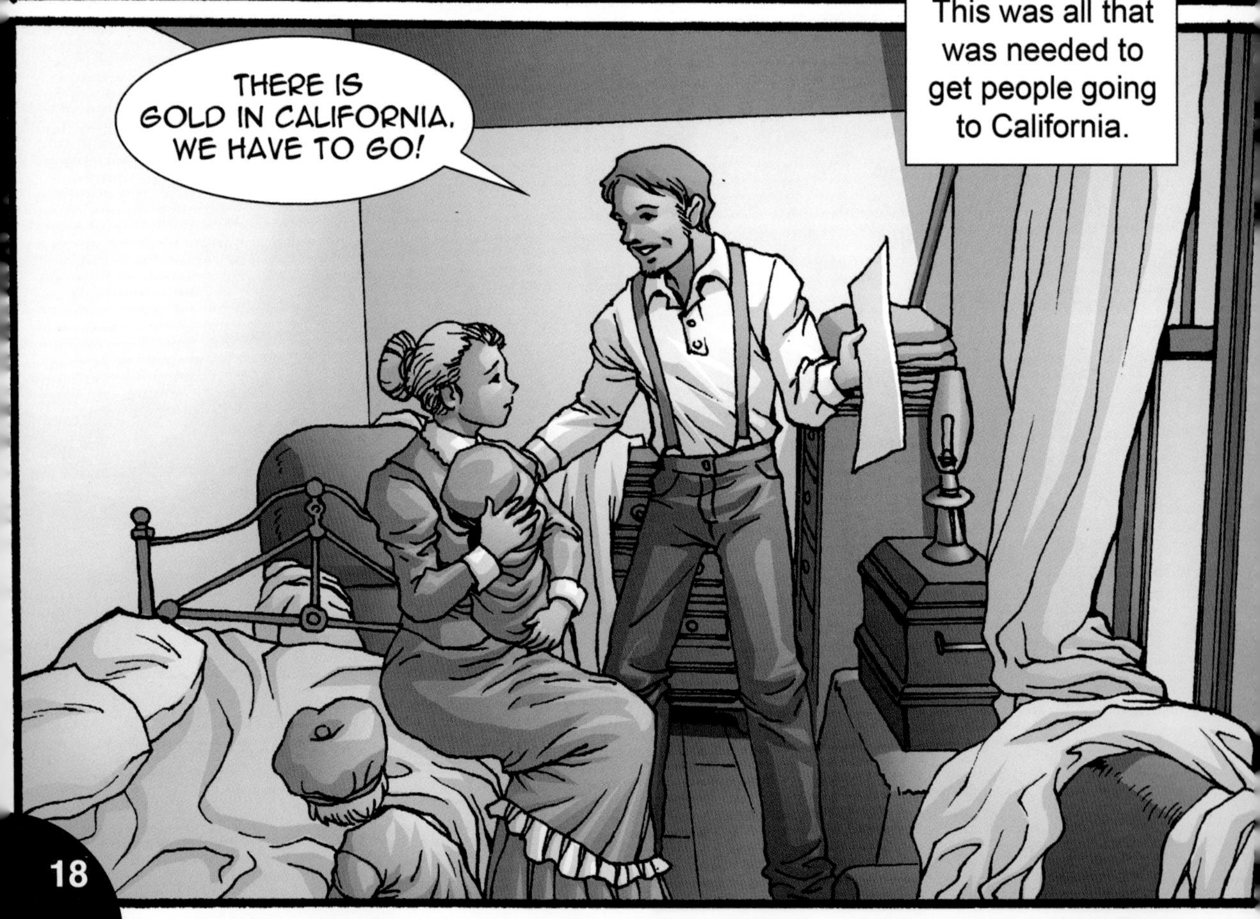

This was all that was needed to get people going to California.
THERE IS GOLD IN CALIFORNIA. WE HAVE TO GO!

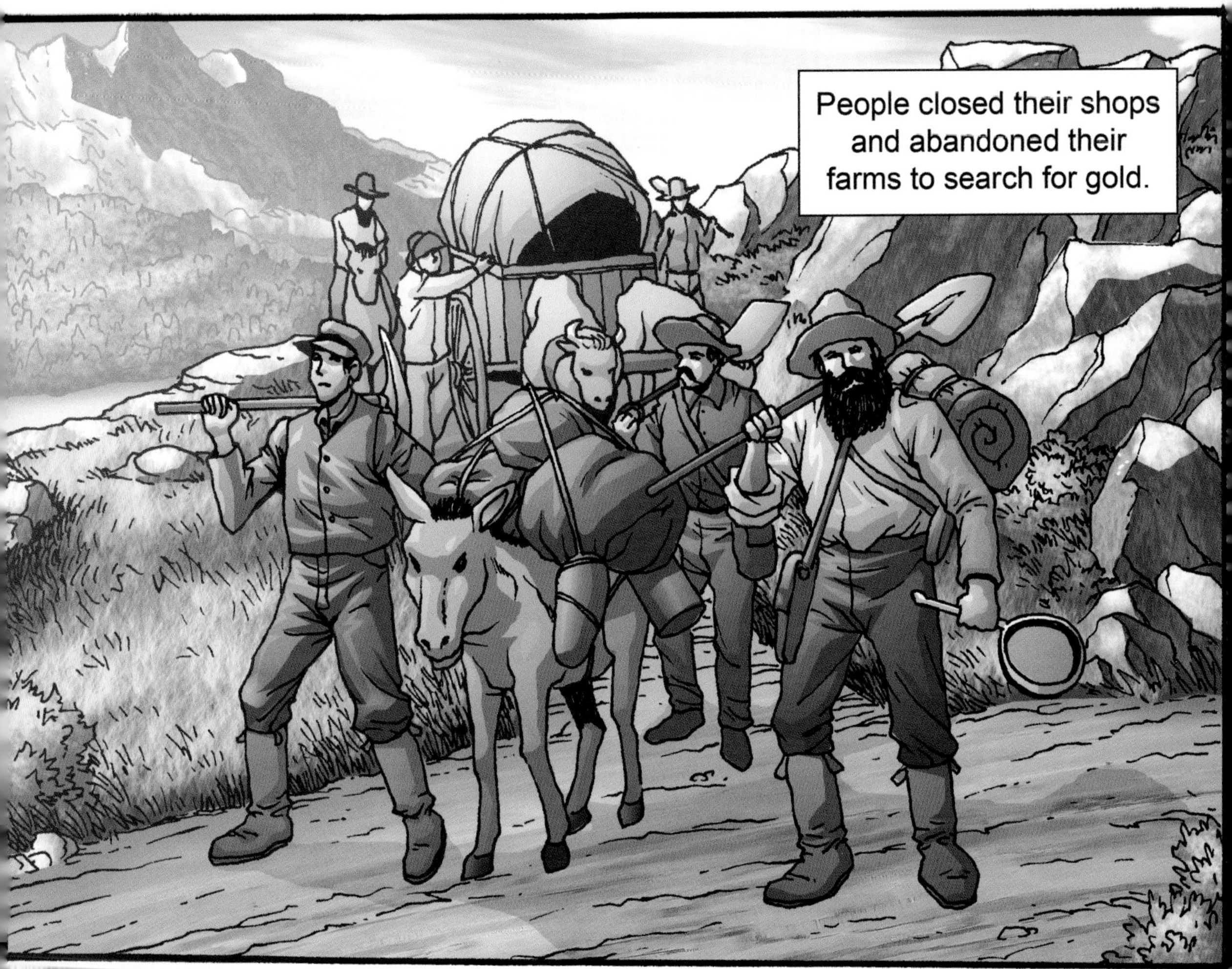
People closed their shops and abandoned their farms to search for gold.

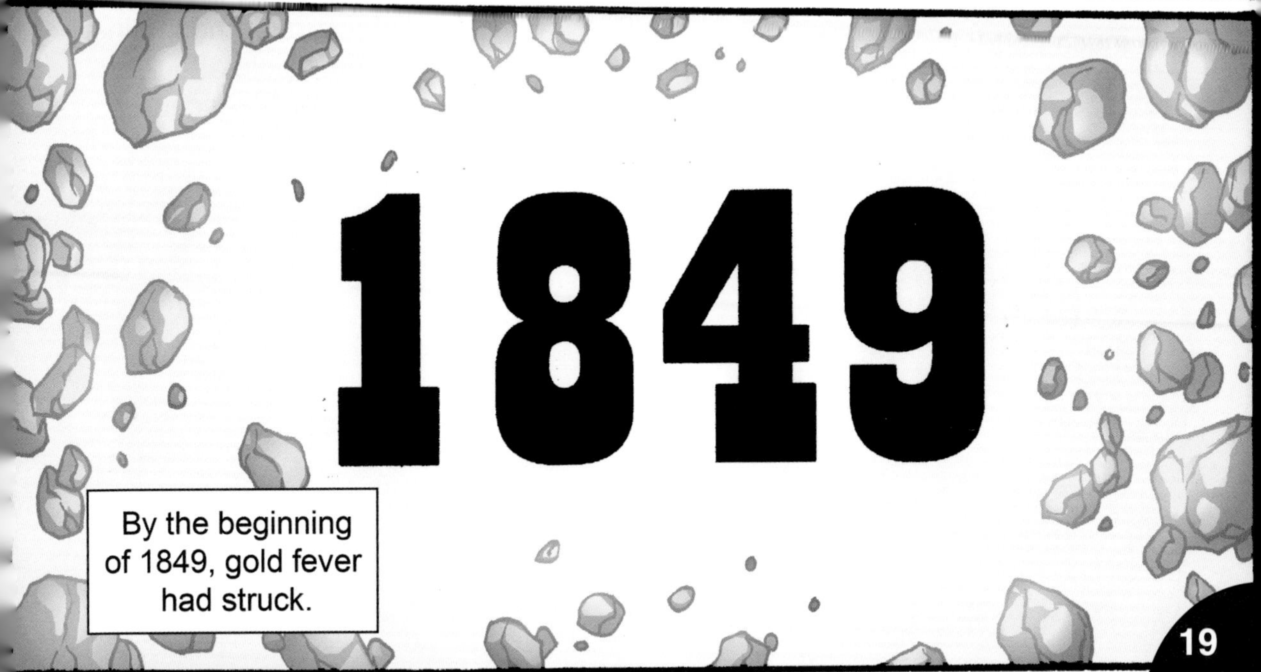
1849
By the beginning of 1849, gold fever had struck.

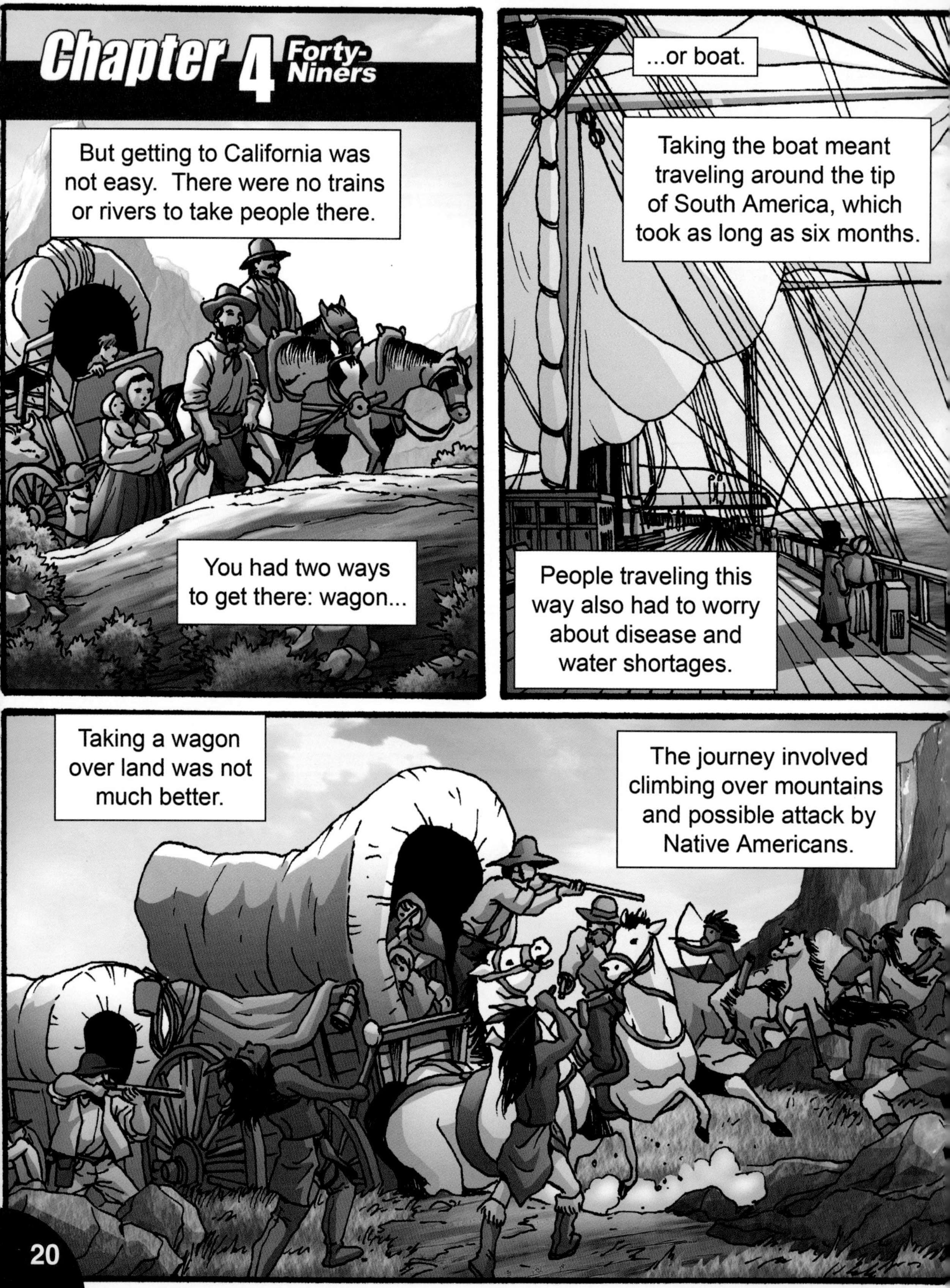
Chapter 4 Forty-Niners
But getting to California was not easy. There were no trains or rivers to take people there.
You had two ways to get there: wagon...
...or boat.
Taking the boat meant traveling around the tip of South America, which took as long as six months.
People traveling this way also had to worry about disease and water shortages.
Taking a wagon over land was not much better.
The journey involved climbing over mountains and possible attack by Native Americans.

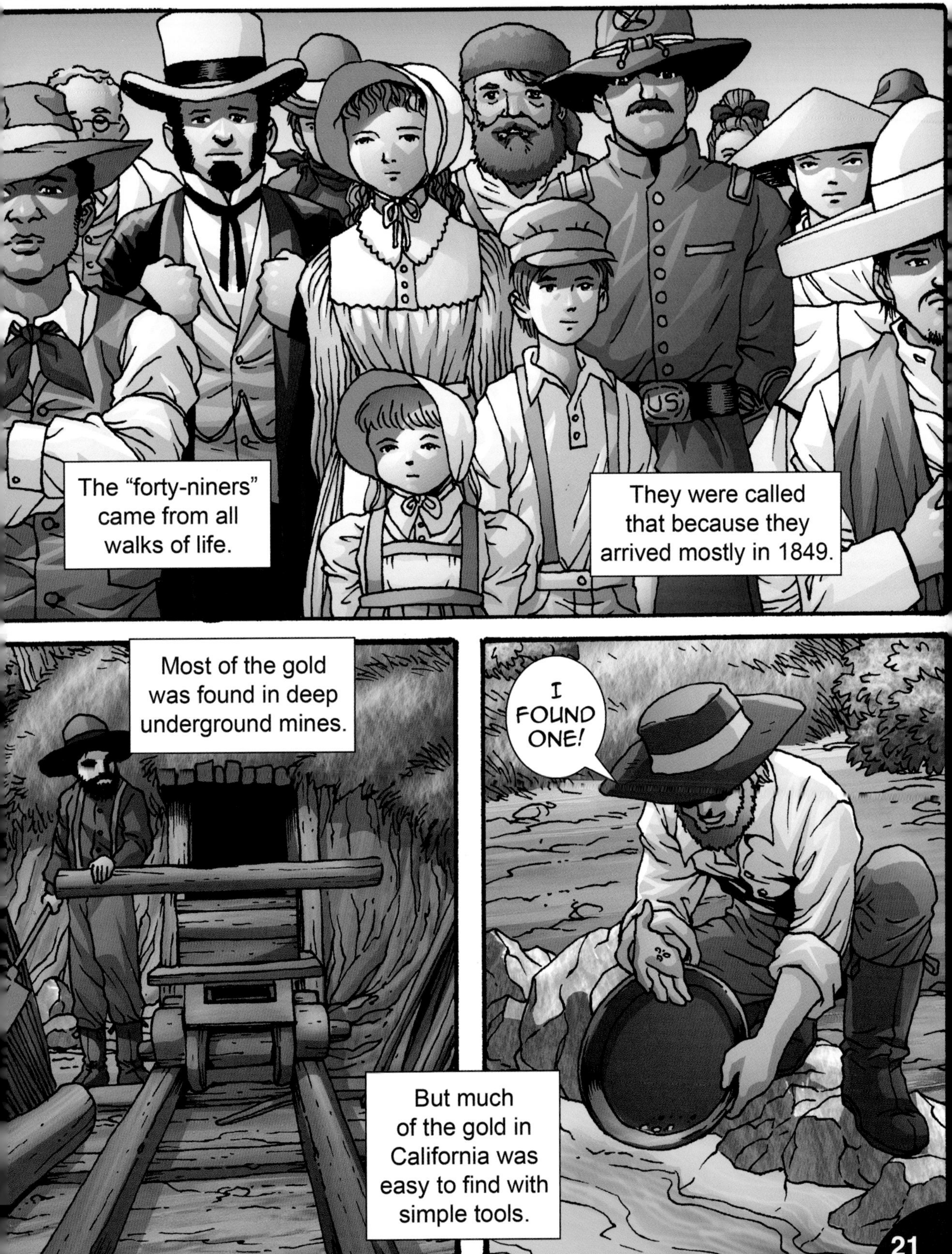
The "forty-niners" came from all walks of life.
They were called that because they arrived mostly in 1849.
US
Most of the gold was found in deep underground mines.
I FOUND ONE!
But much of the gold in California was easy to find with simple tools.

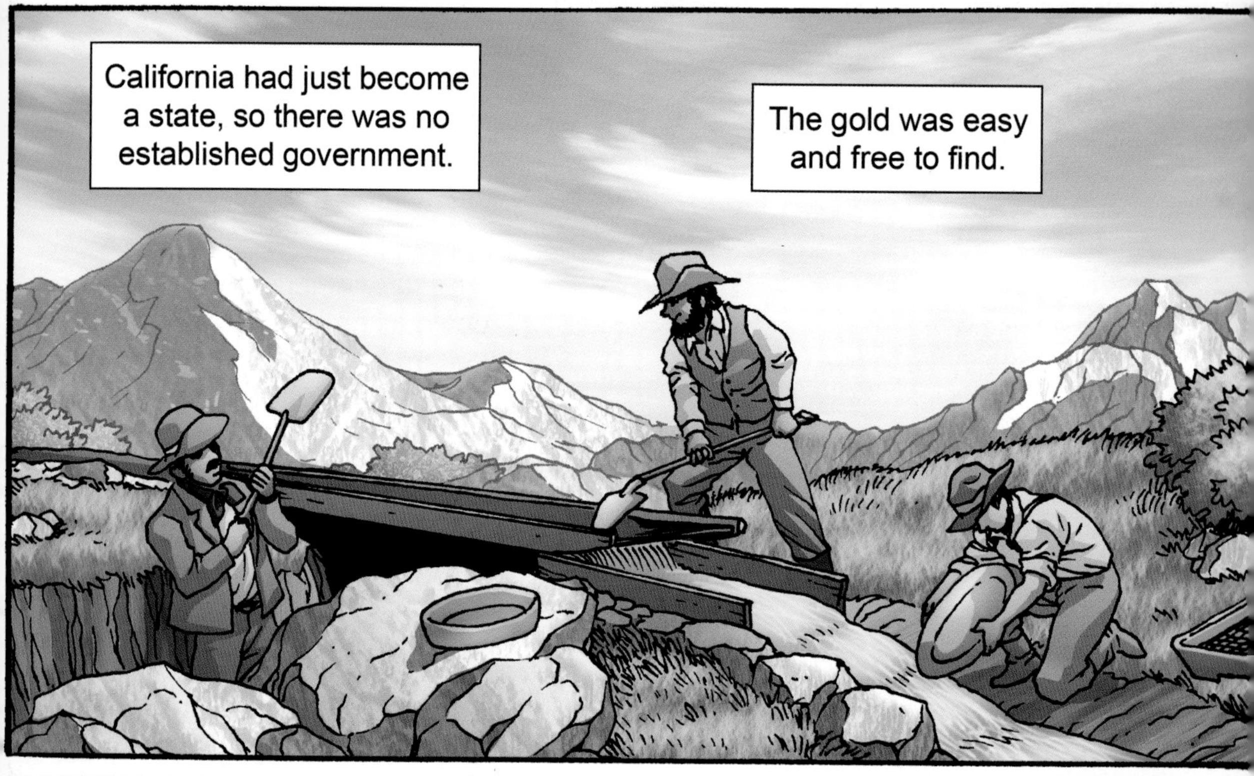
California had just become a state, so there was no established government.
The gold was easy and free to find.

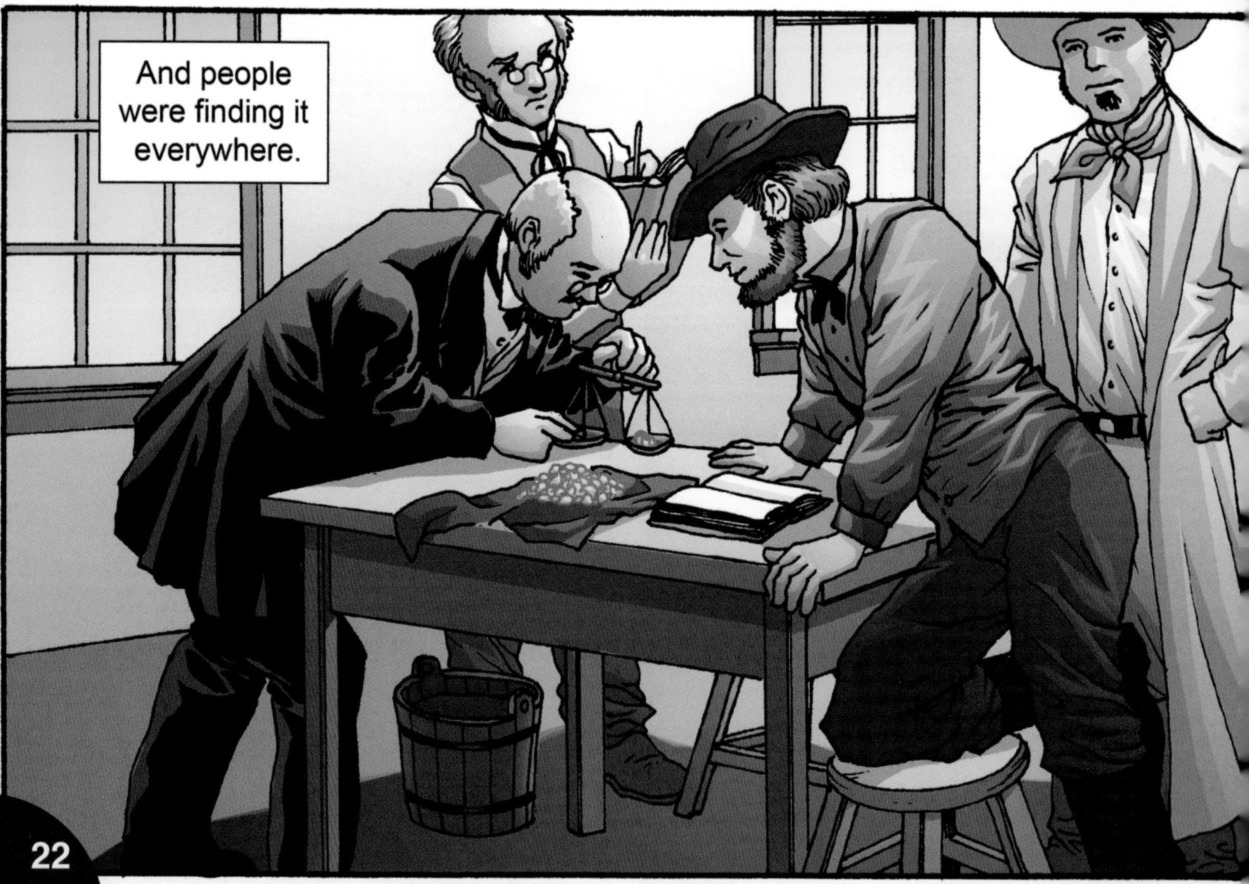
And people were finding it everywhere.

Chapter 5 Supply and Demand

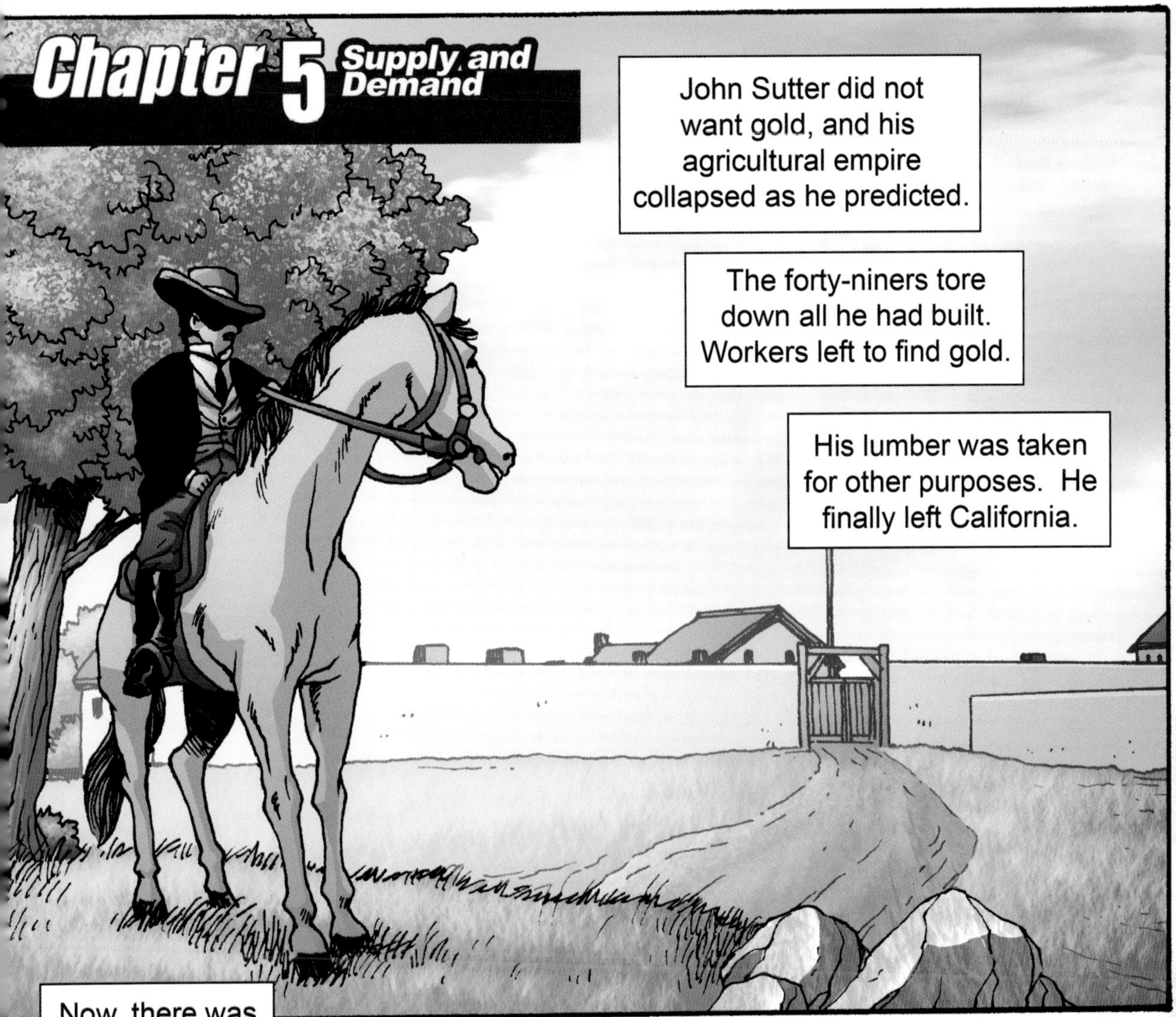
John Sutter did not want gold, and his agricultural empire collapsed as he predicted.
The forty-niners tore down all he had built. Workers left to find gold.
His lumber was taken for other purposes. He finally left California.

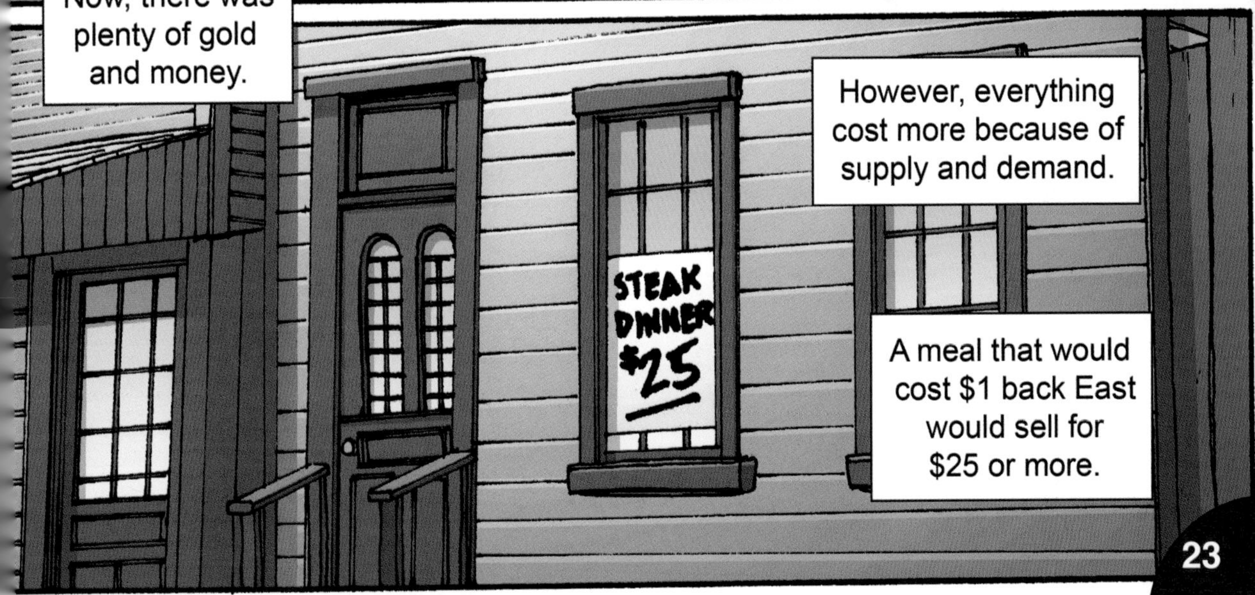
Now, there was plenty of gold and money.
However, everything cost more because of supply and demand.
STEAK DINNER $25
A meal that would cost $1 back East would sell for $25 or more.

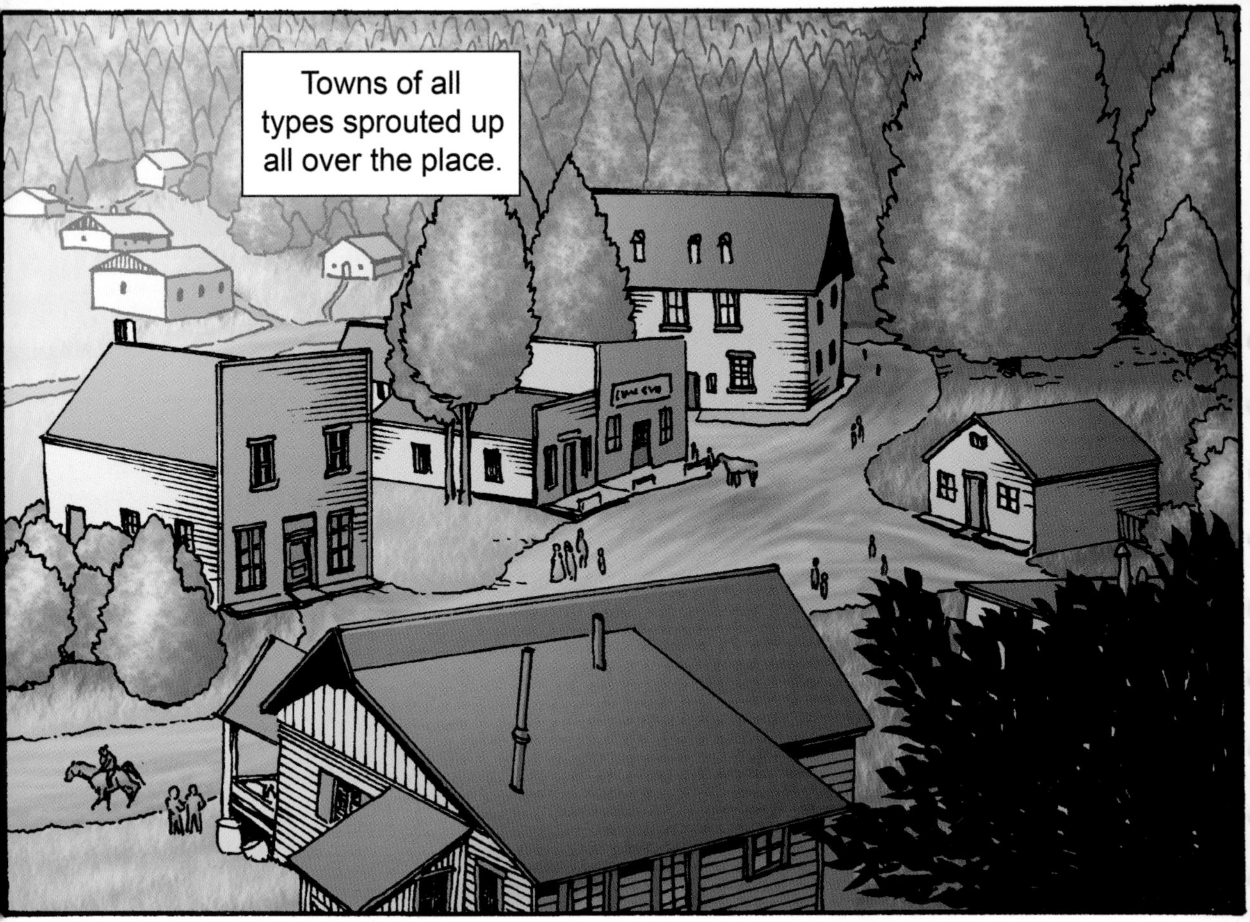
Towns of all types sprouted up all over the place.

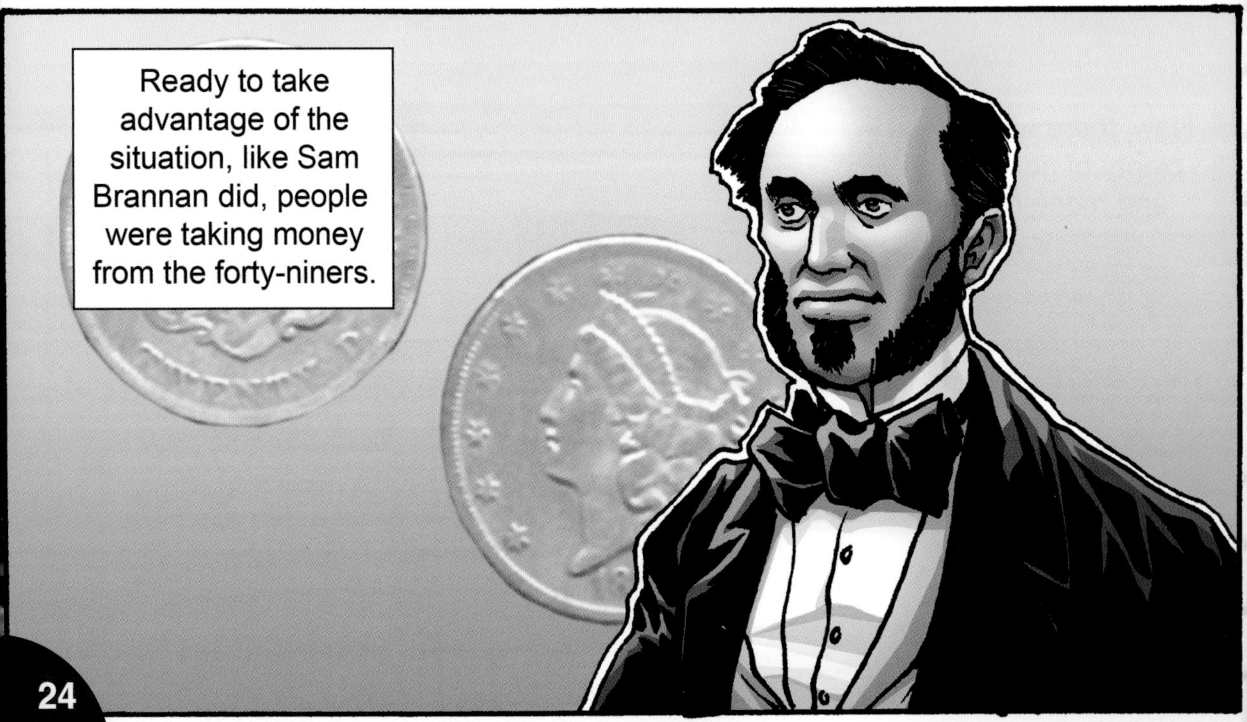
Ready to take advantage of the situation, like Sam Brannan did, people were taking money from the forty-niners.

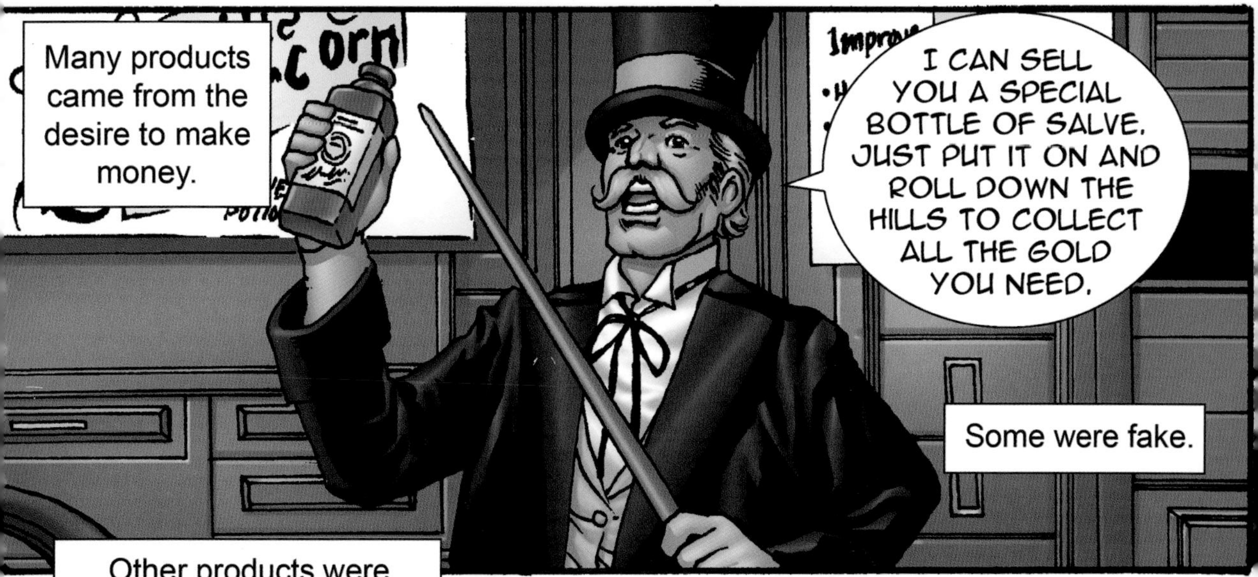
Many products came from the desire to make money.
I CAN SELL YOU A SPECIAL BOTTLE OF SALVE. JUST PUT IT ON AND ROLL DOWN THE HILLS TO COLLECT ALL THE GOLD YOU NEED.
Some were fake.

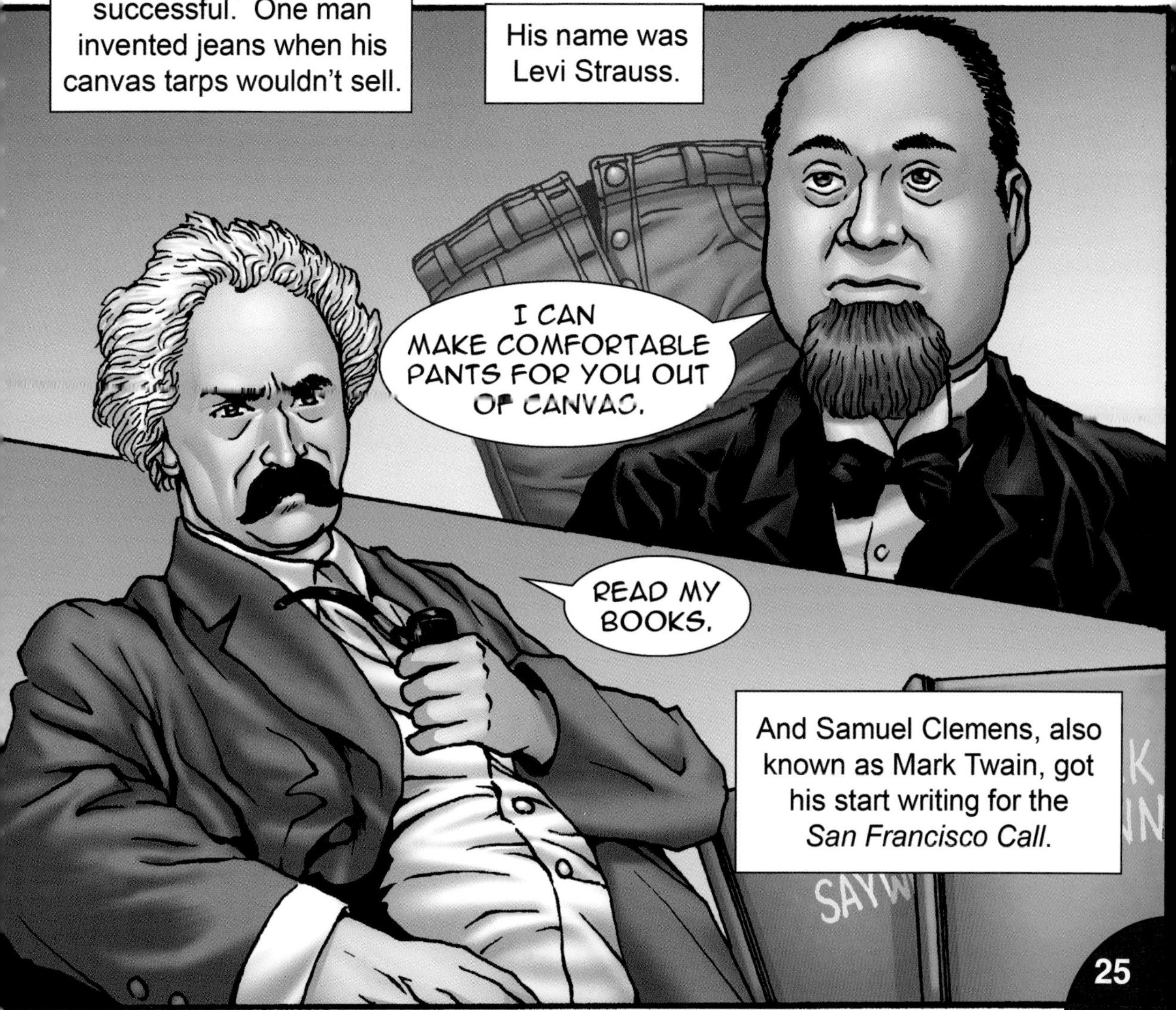
Other products were successful. One man invented jeans when his canvas tarps wouldn't sell.
His name was Levi Strauss.
I CAN MAKE COMFORTABLE PANTS FOR YOU OUT OF CANVAS.
READ MY BOOKS.
And Samuel Clemens, also known as Mark Twain, got his start writing for the *San Francisco Call*.

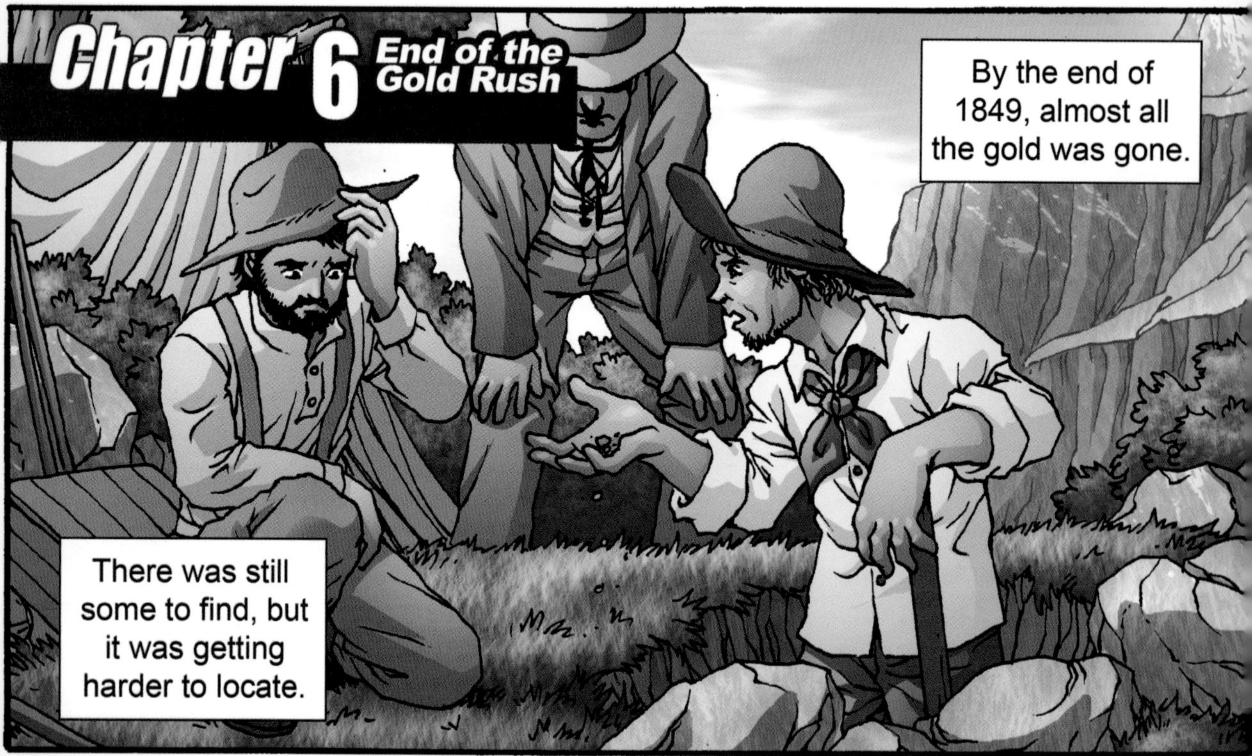
Chapter 6 End of the Gold Rush
By the end of 1849, almost all the gold was gone.
There was still some to find, but it was getting harder to locate.

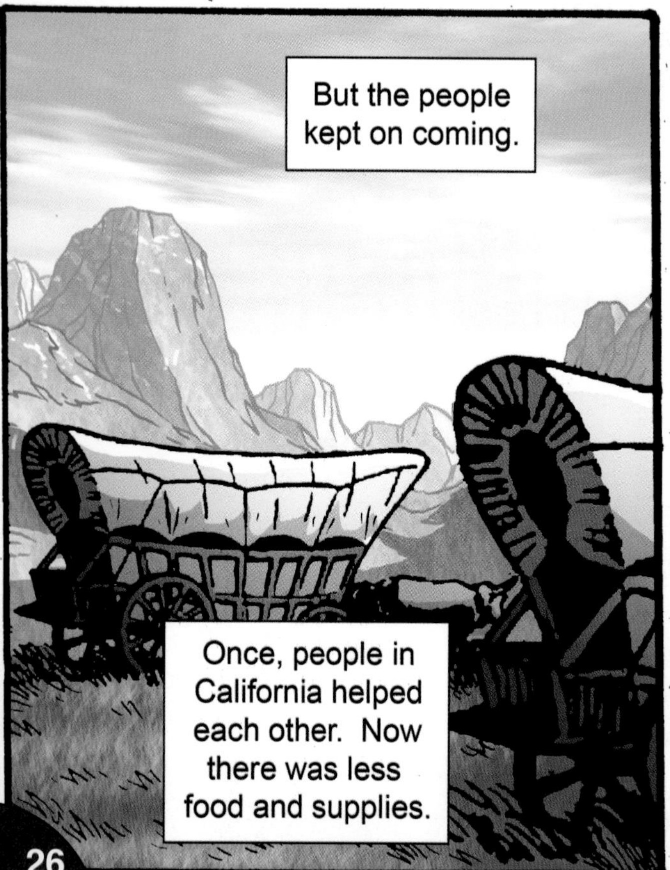
But the people kept on coming.
Once, people in California helped each other. Now there was less food and supplies.

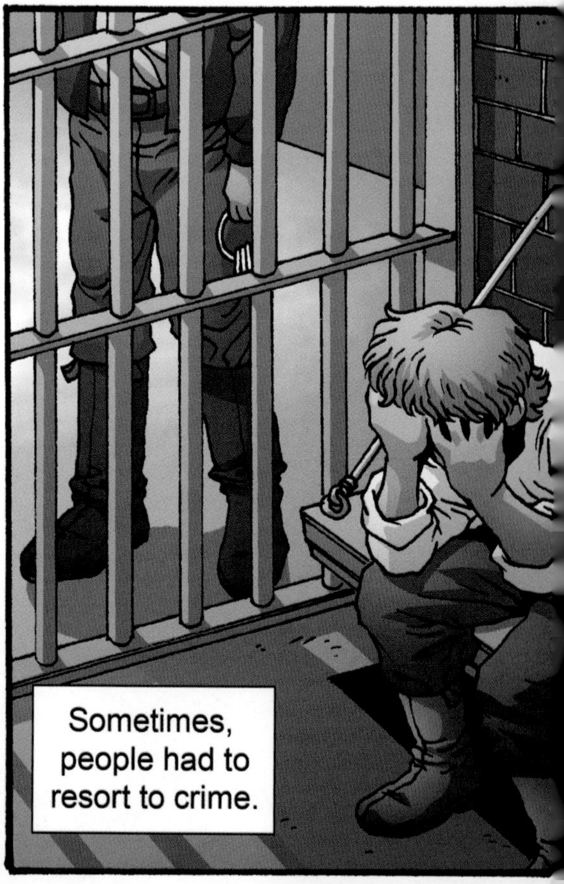
Sometimes, people had to resort to crime.

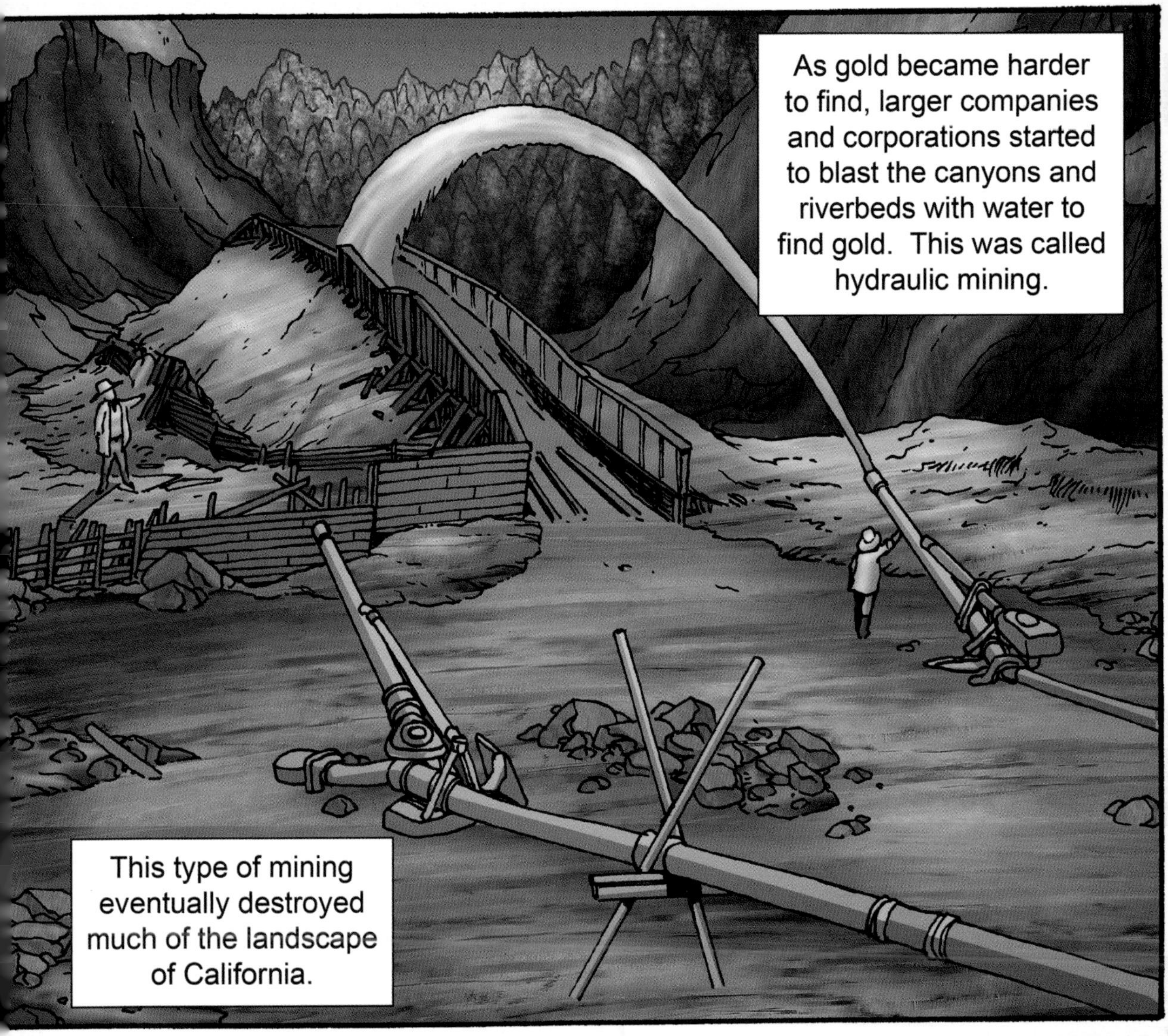
As gold became harder to find, larger companies and corporations started to blast the canyons and riverbeds with water to find gold. This was called hydraulic mining.
This type of mining eventually destroyed much of the landscape of California.

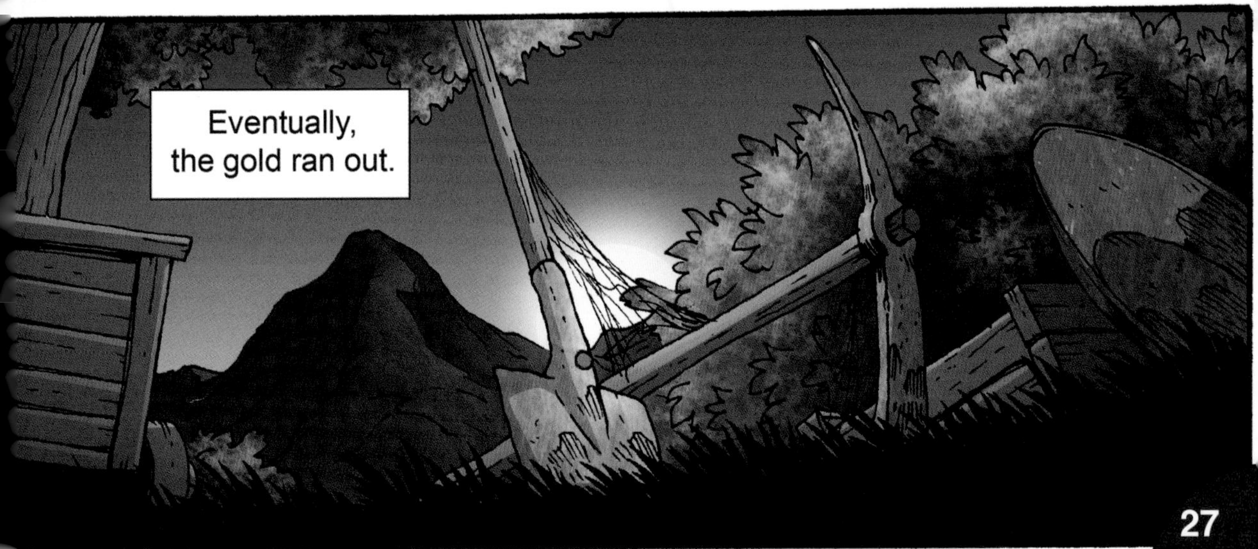
Eventually, the gold ran out.

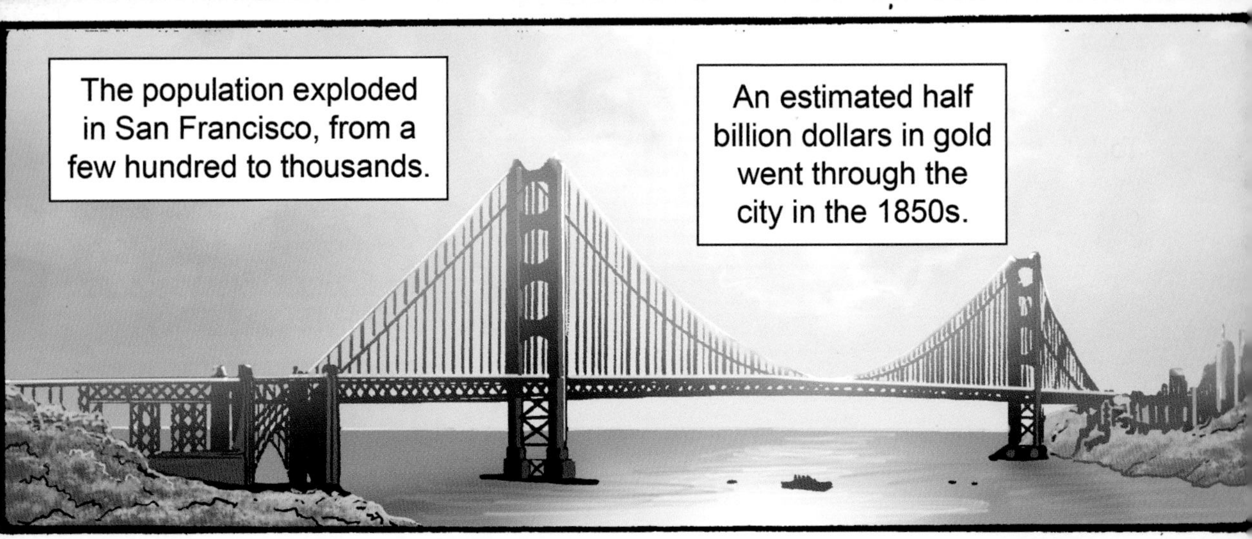
The population exploded in San Francisco, from a few hundred to thousands.
An estimated half billion dollars in gold went through the city in the 1850s.

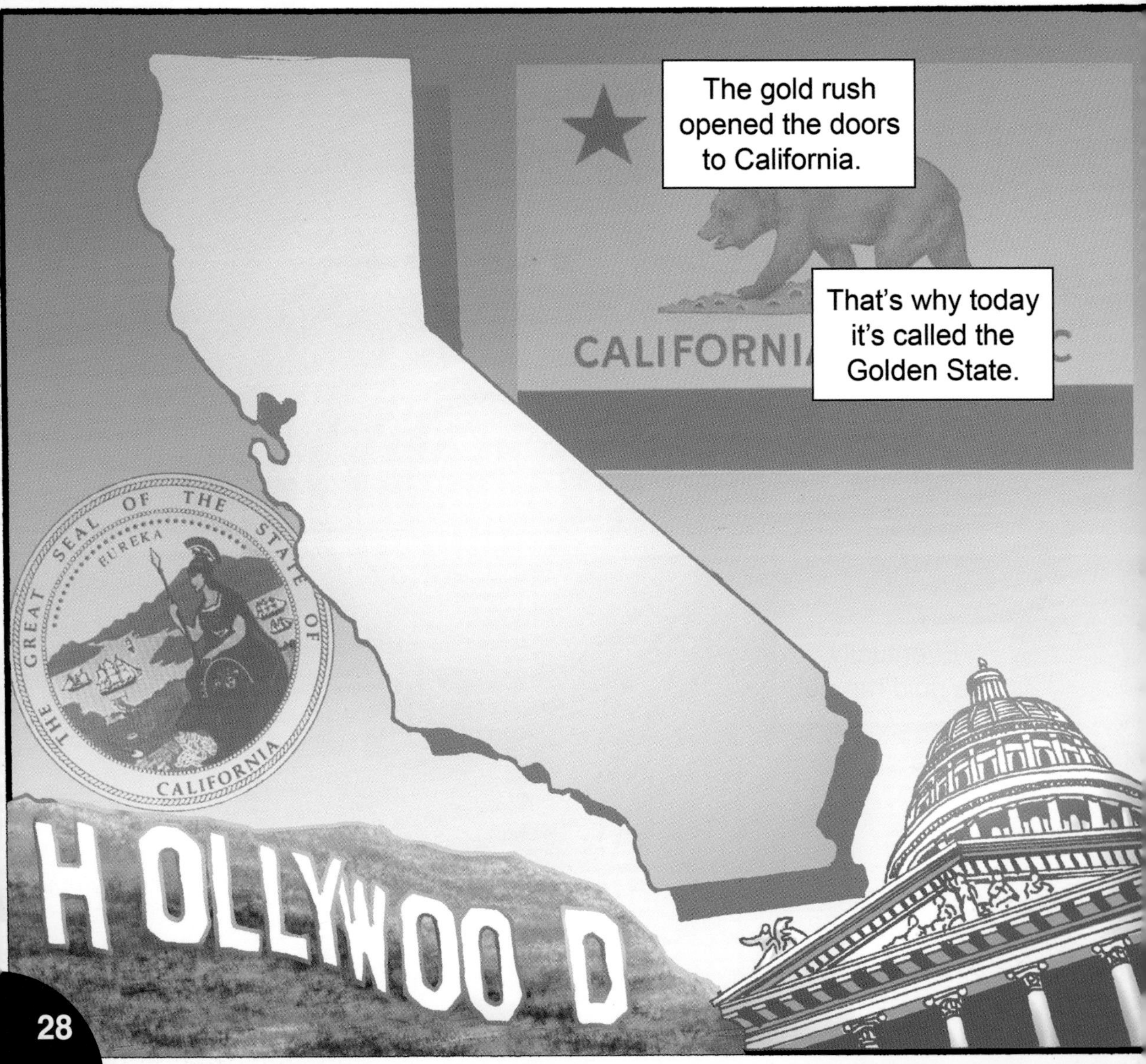
The gold rush opened the doors to California.
That's why today it's called the Golden State.
THE GREAT SEAL OF THE STATE OF CALIFORNIA
EUREKA
HOLLYWOOD

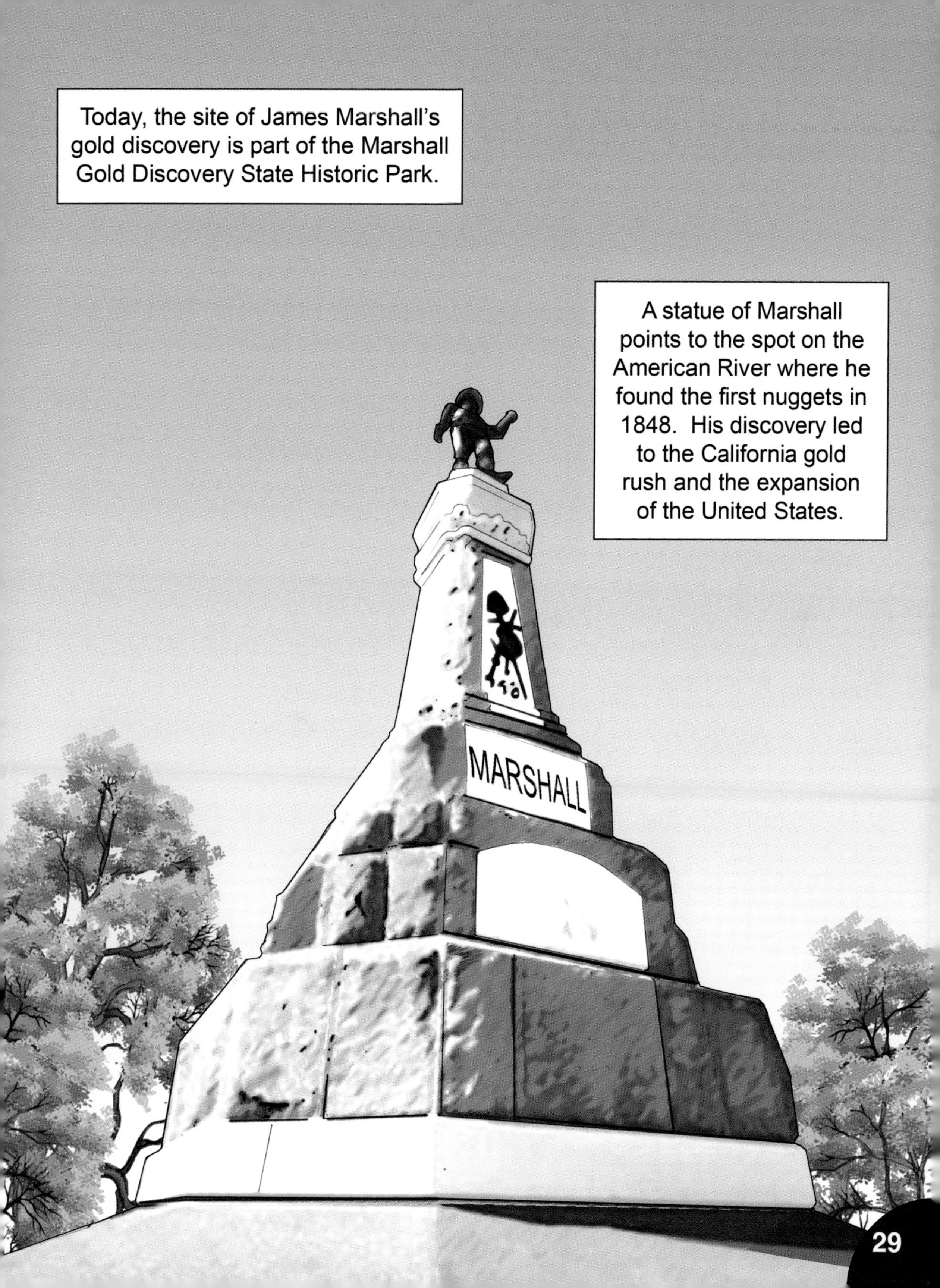
Today, the site of James Marshall's gold discovery is part of the Marshall Gold Discovery State Historic Park.
A statue of Marshall points to the spot on the American River where he found the first nuggets in 1848. His discovery led to the California gold rush and the expansion of the United States.
MARSHALL

California Gold Rush Map

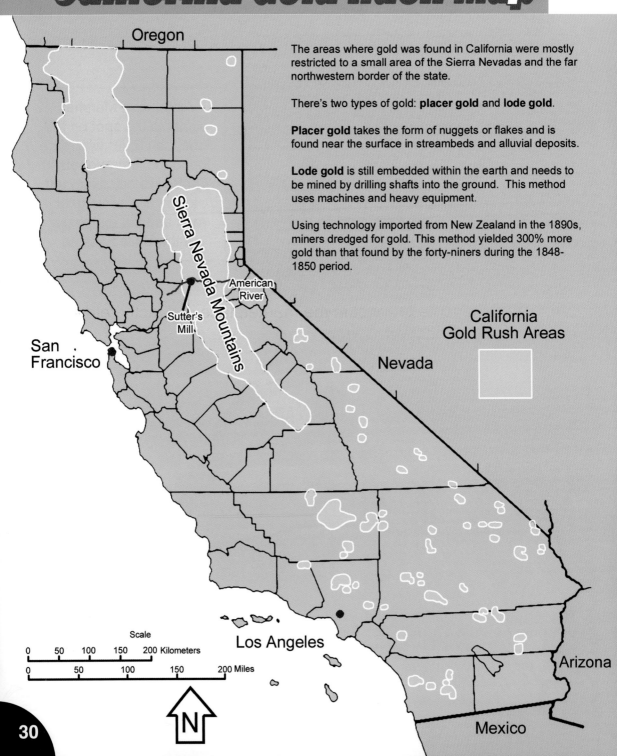

Oregon

The areas where gold was found in California were mostly restricted to a small area of the Sierra Nevadas and the far northwestern border of the state.

There's two types of gold: **placer gold** and **lode gold**.

Placer gold takes the form of nuggets or flakes and is found near the surface in streambeds and alluvial deposits.

Lode gold is still embedded within the earth and needs to be mined by drilling shafts into the ground. This method uses machines and heavy equipment.

Using technology imported from New Zealand in the 1890s, miners dredged for gold. This method yielded 300% more gold than that found by the forty-niners during the 1848-1850 period.

Sierra Nevada Mountains

American River

Sutter's Mill

San Francisco

California Gold Rush Areas

Nevada

Los Angeles

Scale

0   50   100   150   200 Kilometers

0   50   100   150   200 Miles

N

Arizona

Mexico

Glossary

authentic - real.

commission - a request to complete a job or mission.

corroborate - to support by supplying evidence or proof.

domain - area of land owned by a person or government.

speculate - to ponder or review a subject often without coming to a final answer.

supply and demand - an economic principle in which the amount of available product in the marketplace is directly related to consumer demand for it. Often, the price of a product will increase when consumer demand for it exceeds the supply available.

Web Sites

To learn more about the California gold rush, visit ABDO Publishing Company on the World Wide Web at **www.abdopublishing.com.** Web sites about the gold rush are featured on our Book Links page. These links are routinely monitored and updated to provide the most current information available.

Index